MAl

# MANY ROADS

## Women's Personal Stories of Courage and Displacement in Wales

Foreword by Charlotte Williams
Edited by Faaeza Jasdanwalla-Williams
Co-compilers, Chinyere Chukwudi-Okeh and Mohini Gupta

HONNO PRESS

First published in Great Britain in 2024 by Honno Press
D41, Hugh Owen Building, Aberystwyth University, Ceredigion, SY23 3DY

1 2 3 4 5 6 7 8 9 10

A catalogue record for this book is available from the British Library.

Published with the financial support of the Books Council of Wales.

ISBN 978-1-916821-10-1 (paperback)
ISBN 978-1-916821-11-8 (ebook)
Cover design: Ifan Bates
Text design: Elaine Sharples
Printed by 4Edge

This is a work of non-fiction. These are the views of the contributors
based on their personal experiences and are not necessarily a reflection of the
experiences of the entire ethnic group, race or country that they belong to, or
from which they originate. These potentially sensitive experiences should be
considered in context.

Disclaimer: Some names have been changed in order to
protect the identities of contributors and their families.

# Contents

# Foreword

## Professor Charlotte Williams

Migrations in and out of Wales have been a constant feature of this country's history; some are voluntary and some forced. People move to study, for love, for work and other considered choices. But many find themselves in circumstances that compel them to flee their countries of origin and seek refuge. Some experience a mix of the two, choosing to move only to find themselves in unanticipated and exploitative circumstances. Our population is subject to constant flux and change as people arrive and people leave, producing moments of cultural encounter and exchange and prompting transformations in society as a whole. But is this too easy and too romanticised a view of the process? How well do we understand what these movements and displacements entail, how they are lived and experienced, how they are navigated and what they imply, in particular, for women and girls?

The personal stories recounted in this text speak poignantly to the gendered dimensions of such displacement. When people are subject to movement they experience significant losses, perhaps a home, social networks, a role, a career, identities, dreams and prospects, and face significant challenges in new and often strange contexts. You become, says one of the contributors, *'a government entity'* subject to being moved on and moved on ... with no say in what happens to you. There are, however, specific consequences of such disruption for women and girls. Women often bear the additional responsibilities of caring and providing for family members, looking after the mental wellbeing of family members, and may be subject to additional risks of being sexually exploited or subject to violence and abuse. Several of these stories are infused with such distressing details, *'no one should ever underestimate the incredible blessing of being safe and feeling safe'* another contributor tells us.

This cohort of voices, who freely and bravely offer their accounts ended up here in Wales, by design or circumstance. The detail of these stories tell of entering into new social relationships and working through the demands of change and transition in order to reorient their lives and regain agency and control of their circumstances. They take us through the processes of adaptation, all the while with the memory of elsewhere places, times, experiences, the echo of another place providing moments of contrast and comparison with their new homeland. They are simultaneously offering a syncretic experience of here and there, home and away.

And thus we see a picture of Wales as refracted through their lens: the solace and sanctuary of parks, neighbourhoods and landscapes, the Welsh language, a love of *'places that think in more than the eyes of one language'*, new friendships, opportunities taken to share food and stories, feelings of safety returned and skills contributed in 'a two way process' of exchange and integration. What we glean is a diversity of experiences, where ethnicities that emanate from countries across the world form intersections with disability, religious belief, gay sexuality, age and length of residence and of course with Wales itself. These are bold accounts that speak to the unequivocal fact that migrants bring skills, innovations, new perspectives and experiences to Wales, that they are adaptable, courageous and resilient and that Wales has, does, and will benefit from this diversity.

Professor Charlotte Williams
Emeritus Professor Bangor University

# Introduction

## Faaeza Jasdanwalla-Williams

Suddenly all went black. One minute, I was a regular eleven-year-old girl walking back home from school with my classmate, and the next minute, I was on the ground, numb with pain and unable to see anything around me. Apparently, a milk lorry driven by a learner driver had illegally entered our narrow school lane and reversed straight into me. I vaguely recall voices which seemed like they were somewhere in the distance and being rushed to hospital. Whatever the particulars, unbeknownst to me at that specific point in time, my life had altered dramatically in a flash.

I was born and raised in Mumbai (then Bombay), India along with my older brother, by parents who placed the greatest emphasis on educating their two children. However, as a result of my accident, I suffered a brain haemorrhage and lost much of my vision. Now I had to learn to navigate life as a visually impaired child, and my parents had to figure out the best way to ensure that my education would not suffer, even if it meant them having to help me read, write and tackle all my classwork and textbooks throughout school. In fact, my close circle of friends, both on the home front and in school, as well as my teachers, did everything they could to accommodate my needs at a time when there was no access to any visual aids. It was only due to the tremendous determination of my parents and especially my mother, that I not only sailed through school with good grades, but also university with a History degree. My brother too had been my pillar of support, researching all the new advances in technology which would alleviate some of the

3

obstacles I faced on account of my poor vision. The support I received went beyond my immediate family and some of my extended family members became invaluable mentors.

I had undoubtedly imbibed my mother's determination by then and decided to continue my studies in the UK, without my mother's assistance this time, but with the invaluable assistance of my first portable visual aid – a reading machine. The rest, as they say, is literally history, for I studied for a Master's degree in British Medieval History and in due course, a PhD in Early Modern Ottoman History at Aberystwyth University.

I came to Aberystwyth for the first time in 1993 to visit my brother who had been studying there and instantly fell in love with the town. More than the beauty that had enamoured me, it was the idea that this was a town where I could possibly live an independent life without having to rely on others for assistance. In Mumbai, I could not even walk on the pavements due to their unevenness or cross the road on my own, whereas I saw that navigating my way around a small, structured town would be transformative for me.

As it turned out, I also ended up teaching in the Department of History and Welsh History at Aberystwyth University for ten years after completing my PhD and properly began my life here as a full-fledged immigrant, working and supporting myself, contributing like most others, to the system and leading an independent life. However, never for a minute do I forget that if it were not for my parents, I would not even have been able to get through school, leave alone achieve the highest academic qualifications. In fact, my friends and family in Mumbai (not only my brother and sister-in-law, but also my two nieces), and in Wales, have been supporting me and standing by me all along.

Aberystwyth is truly my home now. I met and married the love of my life and have forged a life here, which includes not only friends among the academic fraternity, but also many local, native Welsh people, who welcomed me from the start. Since I harbour a keen interest in learning languages, I made it a point to learn Welsh to a relatively high level and am able to communicate in Welsh to an adequate degree of proficiency. This of course, has further helped me to integrate with the native Welsh-speaking population of Aberystwyth and also provided me with a deeper appreciation of Welsh culture.

Although I have now resigned from my teaching position, as it turned out, just before the world changed on account of the pandemic, I am closely involved with facilitating groups and activities as a volunteer with The Royal National Institute of Blind People as well as with Gwasg Honno.

I am also research active and my secondary academic research revolves around the African Diaspora in India on account of my mother's ancestors arriving in India from the region around what was then Abyssinia, around the fourteenth and fifteenth centuries. Consequently, I have participated closely with events that celebrate the African diaspora globally, especially those in connection with the UN's International Decade for People of African Descent (2015–2024). I had already been extremely disturbed by the general attitude and rhetoric in the UK towards refugees and immigrants in general since the influx of refugees on account of the war in Syria. In 2016, that rhetoric took on a darker tone and it almost became acceptable for people to air their discriminatory views in public. All of this, together with the fact that I was eager to contribute more tangibly to mark the International Decade for People of African Descent, spurred me on towards putting forward a proposal to Gwasg Honno to bring the marginalised voices of immigrant, migrant and refugee women from the periphery to the centre. The absolute need to represent as broad a spectrum of immigrant, migrant and refugee women as possible meant that we, at Honno, decided to not only invite contributions from immigrant, migrant and refugee women from Africa, but also those from Asia, who have now found a home in Wales.

While there has been an increasing interest in reading about and listening to the stories of immigrants, the books that have been published so far largely include people who are already in some way in the public eye, be it TV personalities, sportspersons or writers. In 2019, Malala Yousafzai's book, *We Are Displaced*, comes the closest to what we are hoping to achieve with this book. She related the stories of refugee girls from Yemen, Syria, Iraq, Myanmar and Colombia amongst others, who had fled their own countries on account of political unrest and war, and found themselves displaced in other countries. Her collection highlights the resilience, strength and courage of these girls, as well as the longing they harbour for their homelands at times.

In the UK, books such as *The Good Immigrant*, edited by Nikesh Shukla, published in 2017, discusses race and racism in the UK, bringing into the frame the impact that Brexit has had on the perception of immigrants, migrants, asylum seekers and refugees with the backdrop of a misguided nostalgia for the British Empire, whitewashing all the negative, damaging and disastrous aspects of colonialism. It includes the opinions and experiences of prominent immigrants, first and second generation, of having to navigate life in the UK with the barrier of race before them, rather than being acknowledged and appreciated purely for their achievements and success, irrespective of the colour of their skin.

In 2021, *Seventy Years of Struggle and Achievement* edited by Meena Upadhyaya, Kirsten Lavine and Chris Weedon, brought us the stories of the forty finalists shortlisted for the Ethnic Minority Welsh Women Achievement Awards. This volume emphasises the inspiring stories of women who have shone in their respective fields of achievement, despite the struggles they had to undergo while negotiating a whole new life in Wales. Additionally, 2024 also saw the publication of a collection of stories by immigrant women titled *Gathering*, edited by Durre Shahwar and Nasia Sarwar-Skuse. This collection includes prominent and successful immigrant women in Wales in different walks of life, such as authors, musicians, founders of organisations, etc.

Our diaspora anthology therefore, is not going to be the first book to bring to the fore the stories of immigrant women. But where it differs greatly is the fact that there are hardly any well-known names in the list of female contributors beyond their immediate local communities. Despite this, these women's achievements and lives are equally important and therefore, worth highlighting. I, along with my co-compilers, Chinyere Chukwudi-Okeh and Mohini Gupta, have reached out to women who have hitherto been invisible in the public eye. The main aim of this book has been to highlight marginalised voices as well as voices of immigrant women who have simply been going about their daily lives in a new country, trying to fit in, sometimes struggling with the language of their new home, grappling with a completely different set of cultural norms, traditions and rules. In terms of highlighting marginalised voices, we encountered a number of women who had to flee from their respective countries for various reasons and who have finally managed to find, or are in the process of finding refuge in Wales via the route of seeking asylum. Thereafter, they have been resettled in different parts of Wales through government and local authority schemes and welcomed by local residents, who have raised funds to aid in their resettlement in local communities. This is not a book of women in the limelight, but rather those who are successfully navigating the complexities and nuances of daily life in an alien environment. These are women who are attempting to put the past behind them, despite longing for their homelands and families that they had to leave behind, getting to grips with their new present, and persevering to forge a brighter future for themselves.

The path to forging direct links with immigrant communities throughout Wales has not always been smooth-sailing. While we did receive a few submissions via our website when the call for submissions had gone out, they were nowhere near enough or entirely the sort of contributions we had been hoping for. Furthermore, some immigrant women we did have direct links with, struggled with English and while I speak a range of languages, I was not fluent enough in Arabic or Farsi for instance to be able to conduct interviews in those languages. In fact, in one instance, we did have to engage the services of an interpreter in order to conduct the interview but engaging the services of interpreters for interviews in several languages proved to be impractical and costly. Therefore, recruiting two co-compilers, Chinyere Chukwudi-Okeh and Mohini Gupta (both of whom have also contributed their stories to this anthology), to assist me with contacting individual immigrant women and immigrant communities and setting up interviews for instance, was the turning point for this volume. Each of us contacted women originally from different parts of Asia and Africa that we had links with, and either asked them to write their own story, or set up interviews over the phone or in person with them. In the case of interviews, each of us have written the stories of the women based on their interviews and we have tried to stay true to the tone, manner of expression and sentiment of each individual interview. Even in the editing process, I, as the overall editor of this volume, have been careful not to over-edit each story, precisely to maintain the individuality and distinctness of each experience.

While of course, not every country in Asia and Africa is included in this anthology – indeed, that would have been beyond the scope of a one-volume anthology – we are confident that the anthology is adequately representative of the two continents. From Asia, we have contributions from women from Iraq, Syria, another Middle Eastern country that the contributor has concealed the name of, Afghanistan, Pakistan, India, Bangladesh, Sri Lanka, Malaysia, Japan and China (second generation). From the African continent, we have stories from Algeria, Uganda, Kenya, Namibia, Sudan, Zimbabwe, Zambia, South Africa and Nigeria. Additionally, this anthology also importantly spans the spectrum of experiences, from women who have come into Wales as refugees and who sought asylum, to those who came to Wales as students or accompanied their spouses and then proceeded to acquire qualifications and jobs as well, to those who chose Wales in order to live a healthier, holistic and in general, better life. The full range of contributions further emphasises not only the various countries and cultures that Wales now encompasses, but also the manner in which these new cultures are influencing Welsh society in general, and the local communities in which they live, in particular. Indeed, it is a two-way process. All of these women are at some stage of 'integrating' into their new environments, be it learning new languages, acclimatising to completely different temperatures and weather or then understanding and respecting Welsh cultural norms and customs. In return, they are imparting some of what is the essence of their culture, language, festivals and food, and as a result, they are beginning to feel increasingly welcomed and accepted as the understanding between the cultures grows.

One aspect that has struck me instantly, is that most of these women are contributing to, and participating in not only their local communities, but also the workforce of Wales, either as social workers, carers, university lecturers or chefs. In particular, almost all the refugee women that have contributed their stories, have talked about the deep anxiety and worry they felt after they sought asylum here, in relation to the need to find a job and earn a living for themselves and their families. The incessant rhetoric that is fed to us about refugees not contributing to the system, seems to be entirely misguided, when considering the set of stories from refugee women in this anthology.

It is also important to emphasise that certain opinions expressed by some of the contributors may be rather forthright and therefore, may not always be in keeping with all sensitivities. However, it should also be stressed that these are the views of the contributors based on their personal experiences and are not necessarily a reflection of the experiences of the entire ethnic group, race or country that they belong to or from which they originate. These potentially sensitive experiences need to be considered in context and have been included as our contributors feel strongly that these views be aired.

This anthology then, is simply a vehicle to bring the stories of these strong, courageous, inspiring and enterprising women into the public eye so that they can shine. We need to acknowledge and realise just how Welsh society and culture is being influenced, is transforming and being enriched by these new interactions with the wider world. We should not be looking at a Wales consisting of the native Welsh people on the one hand, and a group of 'other' races and ethnicities on the other, but rather a new, diverse Wales, which is 'integrating' into a more globally sensitive and inclusive society.

Finally, I would like to thank all the women who contributed – those whose stories are included in this anthology as well as those whose contributions we have, unfortunately, been unable to include in this particular volume. We had a limit on the number of stories that we could include in this volume, and we have tried to give voice to those who have never had their experiences published before this. Additionally, in an attempt to be as representative as possible, we have tried to include contributions from as wide a range of countries as possible. I cannot conclude this introduction without expressing my gratitude to BCW for their funding and support, as well as to Chinyere Chukwudi-Okeh and Mohini Gupta for all their assistance and hard work in making this volume a reality.

# Fear and Courage:
# Two Sides of the Same Coin

### Parma

We left our home in Iraq because our lives were threatened. Prior to our departure, my husband held a prominent position within the ruling party of our country. We had a comfortable life, and I was a happy and fulfilled teacher, nurturing the minds of our nation's children. Our own future revolved around our three young children, aged three, two, and one.

One fateful day, an argument within the ruling party escalated into an irreparable divide, leading to a full-blown war. The stronger faction began to persecute and threaten the weaker side, forcing individuals to choose sides. My husband was among those targeted and pressured to align with a particular group.

Initially, we dismissed the threats, hoping they would subside over time. However, the situation escalated into a destructive force that we could no longer ignore. One night, we received a chilling message stating that our children would be taken away if we did not join their party. As devoted parents, we could not allow our children's future to be jeopardised by current circumstances. Unfortunately, not everyone shared the same priorities, and there were those who pursued their ambitions at any cost, even if it meant shedding innocent blood. With such people in power, no corner of our country was safe, especially for a family with three young children.

Faced with no other choice, we made the difficult decision to leave. My husband abandoned his city, his job, and the comfortable life he had built for us. I also left my teaching career and the students

I cherished. We had to leave if we wanted to survive. Through friends, my husband reached out to certain connections, and eventually, an agent was found to help us leave the country. We first arrived in Abu Dhabi and spent a few days there. From there, the agent arranged a temporary visa for us in Belarus, with the intention of eventually reaching Europe.

In Belarus, we lived in hiding, as we did not possess a residence permit. Life was incredibly difficult, lacking even the most basic necessities. Yet, the fear of being caught and sent back home prevented us from seeking help. We decided to venture into the forest, attempting to cross into Poland, despite the harsh winter conditions.

At that time, Poland and Belarus were engaged in a conflict, rejecting people from each other's borders. Regardless of our desperate situation, the political animosity left us stranded. We were trapped, unable to proceed into Poland or return to Belarus. We were stuck, abandoned in a sort of No Man's Land, left to endure the ruthless winter, with no home to return to, no future to look forward to, and no past to turn back to.

Amongst our travelling party of approximately 2,000 people, were those fleeing from war, starvation, persecution, and disease. Many were young individuals travelling alone, and their journey was incredibly arduous. However, for families like ours, with infants and young children, the challenges were even more daunting. We not only had to ensure our own survival but also care for our vulnerable little ones.

The agent had assured us that we would reach Europe within seven days, but as a cautious woman, I had prepared for ten days. We packed necessary supplies such as medication, food, toiletries, and clothes. Unfortunately, after ten days, our provisions were depleted, leaving us at the mercy of strangers who owed us nothing. Perhaps it was the lack of compassion that prevented them from offering assistance.

I saw things in that forest that will forever be etched in my memory. I saw people die because of the cold. I saw children expire because their bodies had become dehydrated, and their kidneys stopped functioning. I saw a pregnant woman pass away from exhaustion and disease. I saw the Belarusian police beat the younger ones among us, asking them to get off their land and go to Poland. I saw despair, pain, and hopelessness.

The Belarusians sent helicopters to fly above us and corral us like cattle. They shouted a message for us saying that we could not return to Belarus and that we had to leave their land. They relayed this message in English and Arabic, indicating that they knew we were people who had come from somewhere from the Middle East, but they could not be bothered beyond simply translating their ultimatum. As the helicopters whirred above us, it felt as though the blades would chop off our heads. The Polish officials also shouted at us through their speakers: 'Do not come near. You must go back. Do not attempt to cross the border.'

Because it was winter, we could not chop wood to make a fire. We had no showers, no extra clothes, and no medicines. My children fell ill, and I was terrified of losing them. My youngest baby cried for milk for two days. I begged everyone, including the Polish guards and the Belarusians for milk. I even offered them $100 for some milk or water for my baby, but they did not oblige.

When we could no longer bear it, we turned to the Belarusians and begged them to let us return. Surprisingly, they allowed us to stay in an alcohol store. The place was a single long hall filled with alcohol, and with no facilities. They simply moved the alcohol to one side while we stayed on the other side. All we had was shelter and a fence around the building. There were no showers, toilets, food, or any other amenities. This was the state of things for four months.

As we emerged from the forest, our troubles began to manifest. While we were in the forest, the authorities sprayed something on us—a reddish powder intended to scare us. I do not know what it was, but I started suffering from blurry vision after they began spraying that substance on us. For my children, the powder caused breathing problems. Everyone in the forest was affected. Although things have improved now since we arrived in Cardiff, my little one still reacts to the cold. She coughs a lot and experiences shortness of breath. Unfortunately, none of the medicines have worked so far.

After four months in that camp on the edge of Belarus, the Belarusian authorities informed us that we had two choices. We could go forward illegally into Poland and then into Germany, where some survived but some did not. The other option was to work with the International Organization for Migration (IOM). They would be coming to speak with us in a few days.

The IOM representatives arrived to discuss our journey and offer us passage back to our home countries. I remember one IOM staff member who could speak Arabic and she said to me, 'You have three young children. Please go back home, go back because of your three children.' But we could not. We had just received a message from Kurdistan saying they knew we would come back, and they would be waiting for us at the airport. The Belarusian authorities said we had to make a decision. So, we agreed with IOM to go to Minsk and then return home. IOM provided us with £5,000 because we were a whole family that had lost everything. However, we did not plan to go back. Our intention was to flee again when we arrived in Minsk.

Upon reaching Minsk, someone from the IOM listened to our story and told us they understood our plight. They asked us not to return to Iraq, as they had heard stories of people who fled, returned and then came back to try to enter Europe through another border. The IOM assisted us by providing a place to rest and recover. After we had recovered, it was time to move again.

Some families chose to return to their home country. One of the families that made this decision did so because the mother in the group had cancer, and her family feared that she would die. They preferred to return home so that their mother could spend her remaining days in a familiar place and receive a proper burial.

After we had rested once again, we contacted our agent. Despite having deceived us before, our desperation to reach Europe led us to engage him once more. He claimed to know a better route to Europe if we could provide him with additional funds. We reluctantly agreed.

The agent arranged for someone to assist us, promising us that this person knew a way to cross the border into Poland. Under the cover of darkness one night, I secured my youngest baby to my chest, and we began our journey. The new route was less heavily patrolled, but it presented significant dangers. It led us through a treacherous swamp where we witnessed people succumbing to its perils, while we clung to hope for our own survival. On several occasions, I narrowly escaped falling to my death, but thanks to my husband and two other men, I was pulled to safety. The same fate befell my husband. Whenever we failed to cross successfully, we returned to wait for another nightfall and attempt the journey again.

After ten attempts, I pleaded with my husband to consider going back. Our lives were not secure here, just as they were not safe back home. However, the situation was worse here due to the lack of identity. If we were to die here, we could be buried in the swamp or in some shallow grave like common criminals. Returning home, would at least ensure a burial in our own land with some dignity if we were killed.

That night, the agent begged us to try once more. It was during the eleventh attempt that we finally set foot on Polish soil. However, our moment of relief was short-lived, as we were immediately arrested by the Polish authorities for crossing the border illegally. We faced a trial conducted in an online court, and my entire family was sentenced to six months in prison. When I raised the issue of sending a one-year-old child to prison, I was met with the response that the law was the law.

The prison authorities confined us to a small, amenity-free room. There were no toilets or running water, leaving us unable to shower or access necessary medications. Our meals consisted of one piece of stale bread per day, and at times, they offered us pork. As Muslims, we abstain from consuming pork due to religious reasons, but our hunger, malnutrition, and exhaustion left us with no choice but to eat it.

We were allowed only twenty minutes of communication with our families in a twenty-four-hour period. Our families had been traumatised by not knowing what had happened to us, so they were relieved to hear from us. However, the presence of Polish guards nearby during our phone calls restricted us from speaking freely. We were warned that they were listening, and any negative remarks about the situation or about them would result in us being barred from leaving forever.

One day, a charity visited the prison to provide assistance. They brought food, toiletries, clothes, soap, and comfort. When they asked me what I needed, I simply said, 'I just want milk for my children.' The charity then provided milk for my babies and some food for us. My children had cried for milk for days and my heart had broken with each cry they uttered and each tear they shed. I had looked at myself and my husband. We had a life in Iraq. I had a job. My husband had a political career. And suddenly, we were out here in a strange land, in prison, begging for food and milk and being served stale bread and pork.

One day, the police came to us and told us we could leave in two days. In two days, they returned our mobile phones and all our personal effects which they had confiscated. They showed us an open camp and told us we could stay there for six months, move to another country if we wanted or be screened for asylum. We did not screen for asylum. We did not want to stay in that country. We had suffered enough. So, with our remaining money, we found another agent – a Turkish man who had a taxi. He drove us from Poland to Dunkirk in France. We stayed in France for five days. Then, we took a small boat across the water into the UK. Our journey lasted about four hours. But it was not without its hiccups. Our small boat ran out of petrol in the middle of the sea. I sat with my children, wondering if we had survived a desert, a forest, a swamp, imprisonment, forbidden food and an uncertain drive only to come and perish in the sea so close to freedom. How could life be like this? I was thinking these thoughts when a big boat belonging to the UK authorities came to rescue us. The officials on the big boat were kind. They gave us food, water, blankets, milk and played with the children. I saw my children smile for the first time in a long time, so I smiled too. After that, they took us to Croydon, where they fingerprinted us. After the fingerprints, they put us in a hotel in London for a month. After that, they sent us to Cardiff, where we stayed in a hostel for six months. Then they sent us to Swansea.

We are safe now. There are no more forests, swamps, camps, prisons, or death. But we remember it all. My children remember everything. Every time we go sightseeing in Swansea, my children cry at the rustling of a leaf. I see fear come into their eyes when they see someone they have not seen before. They still cough uncontrollably when they take a cold bath, and the younger ones cry when their older sibling goes to school. My body remembers too. My vision is still blurry from the powder that was sprayed in the forest between Poland and Belarus. I still shiver when I remember what we went through to get here. I remember how my children learnt to talk in prison. I remember that I was forced to eat pork in Poland against my will.

We are safe now; the UK government sends us some money every week. We are receiving counselling and I am attending English classes to gain knowledge of the language.

We are safe now; we are settling in slowly but steadily. One of my children attends school, and the others will soon follow.

We are safe now, and I am dreaming of giving something back to this country that has accepted us with open arms.

We are safe now.

*Our special thanks go to Shahsavar Rahmani for assisting in translating Parma's story during our interview with her.

# *Hiraeth,* Queeraeth

## Devika Karnad

*Mae hiraeth arna i am Bombay.* Not a longing for the city of Mumbai that exists today on the Western *Ghats* (mountain range) of India, but the one I left behind six years ago when I got on a plane for Cardiff to begin my PhD. The one that held my Ammama (grandmother) in it, the one that had not been ravaged by COVID-19, the one in which I was deeply attached to my family because they were the centre of my life, and the one in which I spoke four languages on a daily basis.

That swift movement between Hindi and Konkani, Marathi and English, in my conversations at home was the reason I chose Cardiff as my new home in the UK – because I only know how to exist in places that think in more than one language. A signboard that is written only in English seems empty to me, haunted by its missing companion, uncomfortable in the inability to cross-check the information in a different script. In my first term at Cardiff University, I decided to learn Welsh so that the pleasure of existing around the language of my new home could grow into familiarity. I learnt to say that I like coffee, and that I study literature, and that the *hiraeth* (longing) is upon me for a true sense of home.

I did not need to learn Welsh fluently to start to feel at home in Wales – that sense of contentment was found by spending time in nature. My oasis lay in the centre of Cardiff city, in Bute Park, where I spent entire mornings strolling through its most wooded, secluded bits, or sitting on a fallen log before a softly tinkling stream to contemplate the twists and turns of my life so far, or cosying into a patch of grass on a sunny day with a favourite book (usually my unedited collection of Jane Austen's letters) and watching the dogs and children gleefully pursue their colourful balls. When I sat in a bus or train and watched the green undulating Welsh hills fly past, I felt a tug upon my heart that pulled me closer to falling in love with the country. I began to associate the open-skied beauty of the Welsh countryside with the vistas of freedom that faced me now, as I found the space to expand into my own self.

Back in Bombay, there was no space to find the contours of my identity while cradled within my close-knit nuclear family life. In that loving home, my individual choices and desires were tolerated, but they could not supersede the choices and desires of the family, or the community. We ate together at certain times of the day, we dressed respectfully, we kept our political opinions to ourselves, we did not lose ourselves in reading a book when a family member wanted to converse with us, we went to all the family events irrespective of whether we knew anyone there, and smiled respectfully when far-off relatives asked intrusive questions about our personal lives, and we did not question decisions made on our behalf. Now, in my terribly small room in Wales's oldest women's hall of residence, Aberdare Hall, I began to learn who I was. I learnt that I like batch-cooking and Welsh cakes, and could happily eat mushrooms for every meal of the week; that I like a leisurely shower of an evening after the day's work is done, rather than conforming to the routine of the household in Bombay, which forced me to bathe at a specific time each day. I discovered that I am not a night owl and I only stayed awake all night in Bombay because it was the only time I could find solitude in a bustling house. And I learnt that I identify as queer.

Cardiff became the home to my newly discovered queerness because this identity could not exist in Bombay. Its presence in that family home had the potential to destroy relationships; it would supersede the traditional route to happiness that my parents envisioned for me in which I settled with a young man of their choice from the community. Acknowledging my queerness would mean choosing the hardest path – one that was lonely because I knew almost no queer people in India and had no access to a community, at least not one that would not be strewn with the disappointed hopes and dreams of parents, and the thorns of the disdaining gossip of far-off relatives. How would I face these hurdles? How could I throw away the stable foundation of my life and walk away for the sake of a new identity I did not yet know much about?

And so, when I first had an inkling of my being queer, when I could not even face it myself, I hid it away in the corners of my room in Cardiff, stashed into the pride flag hanging above my desk until I was ready to come out to myself, and to my family. Years of hemming and hawing passed, punctuated by my emotional but firm refusals of my parents' offer to begin looking for an arranged match for me. They could not understand why this conversation made me weep, and I could not tell them why, because I did not even fully accept it myself. But the bud of self-discovery that was sown early in my new Welsh life did finally blossom when I identified to myself as lesbian in the early hours of a morning in 2021. While the country was weaving in and out of lockdowns, I burst into the open with my queer joy at last.

And I found that this queer joy was welcomed in Cardiff. I was led by the hand by one of my very best friends into the arms of an accepting, loving, celebratory queer community at the heart of Cardiff. On my first day of being out as lesbian to myself and a close group of friends, I made my first visit to the Queer Emporium – a wonderful community space that sells books, gender-affirming clothing and pride clothing, pride flags and badges, and the most colourful, camp drinks and food. I bought a book by the Welsh novelist Sarah Waters whose stories, set in the Victorian period, feature lesbian protagonists. Here, I could display my identity safely, sitting on the bench outside the Queer Emporium with my unicorn cupcake and bisexuali-tea, discussing queer theory with my best friend.

In the two years since this first coming out, I have immersed myself in the queer spaces in Cardiff. I have attended film screenings and book launches at Queer Emporium, cheered on a host of queer performers at the Big Queer Picnic every year at Pride Cymru, spent time on weekends taking in the art exhibitions and browsing the book collections at the neurodivergent, queer-led community library at Dyddiau Du, attended creative writing workshops focused on queer Welsh history at the St. Fagans museum, and enjoyed the LezDiff film festival organised by Chapter Arts Centre. There is more yet for me to discover – this year, I want to go to the pride event organised by Glitter Cymru, a group that supports the ethnically diverse LGBT community in South Wales and hosts regular meet-ups and events. I want to visit the Queer Emporium's newly opened events space in Cardiff's city centre, Enbys ... and I hope the list will continue on as more homes for queer hearts are built into this city.

The homeliness of Wales for my queer self became more rooted when I met and promptly fell in love with a wonderful *Cymraes* (Welsh woman). With her, my journey of falling in love with Wales, and with myself in Wales, has culminated. She roots me in the history of this country, telling me stories from the *Mabinogi*, conjuring scenes that took place in Welsh castles five centuries ago, and patiently helps me translate the Welsh sentences from my beginner's book. Together, we visit Anglesey's beaches, and the coal mine in Blaenavon, and I read the Welsh signs and repeat the Welsh train announcements over and over as we travel to these parts of Wales, while she corrects my pronunciation. We watch *Pride* (2014) together and she tells me more about the LGSM alliance (Lesbians and Gays Support the Miners) that supported the Welsh miners' strikes in the 1980s. We go on after-dark tours of Caerphilly Castle and she fills me in on its connection to King Edward II and his lover Hugh Despenser. We take day trips to the towns in Wales that are important to her family. We drink tea in the tearoom she visited on weekends with her grandfather and her uncle in Abergavenny. We look for fossils on Penarth beach, just like she did as a child with her father.

Home is now the life my partner and I are building in the Welsh valleys, while Bombay is reduced to the city I grew up in and grew out of. That metropolis is engulfed in the sadness of change, both its own and mine. I could not visit it for two years during COVID lockdowns, and in that interim, my grandmother who was the most stable entity at the centre of our familial universe, as well as of my world in Bombay, passed away. I could no longer expect to return home and find a box of my favourite Mangalorean snack – *bubus rotis* – lovingly made by her waiting for me. I would never again spend a slow afternoon in her living room after a warming, traditional Konkani meal, listening to her gossip with my mother and aunts. The house that I entered excitedly as a child, awaiting a weekend of fun with my cousins who all congregated there, was now bereft of the presence that pulled us all to it. The softness of her touch, her voice, her cotton saris, which made home, home, all disappeared in an instant, while I was stuck 3,000 miles away. The wrenching unfamiliarity with 'home' caused by this loss is only compounded by the city's constant transformation. Bombay is a city obsessed with ambitious growth; every few months, a new bit of construction sprouts from its bowels. Since I lived there six years ago, a serpentine metro line has raised itself in front of our apartment complex, making the terrain of home unrecognisable. When I returned to Bombay in early 2022 after more than two years away, there was a sense of being untethered, unrooted.

I cannot, however, place blame on the city's metamorphosis alone. In these six years, I have admittedly undergone a similarly ambitious transformation, and my grief for the old sense of homeliness I felt in Bombay is largely entwined in the feeling that who I am is not acceptable in that city and its country. A month before I cheered on the sidelines of a colourful pride parade through Cardiff last year, the government of India argued in the Indian Supreme Court that same-sex marriage is entirely against Indian tradition. It is Cardiff and Wales that now represented comfort, familiarity, and safety to me, while Bombay felt hostile. My home in Adamsdown first became a safe haven through COVID as both India and England struggled through far less responsible COVID rules, which resulted in a meteoric rise in infections. Ironically, it was COVID that strengthened a sense of Welsh identity when the devolved Welsh government became responsible for COVID guidelines in Wales and chose often to depart from the path taken by the central UK government. The Welsh border felt more solidified as traffic between England and Wales was monitored, and there was a sentiment of self-preservation within the country from the possible damage its neighbour might cause if the border remained fluid. While concerns about COVID transmission diminished, this safe haven remained one for me as I embarked upon my queer journey mid-pandemic.

So it is, that *hiraeth* has come upon me for that first home of Bombay, lost to me in so many tangible and intangible ways. Instead, I am left with the remnants of my Bombayness that awakens to the smell of petrichor when rain descends upon a hot day near Caerphilly; or when I teach my partner a phrase in Konkani as we cook *aloo gobi* or garlic *dal* or *vada pav* in the kitchen; or when I painstakingly source Alphonso mangoes from Nasik to eat in a tiny Welsh village, our mouths sticky from the dripping golden juice. But through these tethers to my old life, I am slowly beginning to reconnect with the bits of Bombay that bring me joy while safely cocooned in this home where I can freely be queer and Welsh.

From my spot on the yellow couch in my partner's home in the Welsh valleys, I am beginning to explore the queer communities I can find in India, that are bravely waving the pride flag in the face of cultural and political opposition. I am witnessing the beauty of queer Indian couples getting married even though the law will not allow it, of the parents who have the courage to come out as allies and march with their children at pride events in different Indian cities, of the trans activists using their visibility on social media to stand up for their community despite the barrage of hatred they might receive. I am finding validation in Saleem Kidwai and Ruth Vanita's incredibly well-researched tome *Same-Sex Love in India: Readings from Literature and History*, which records the existence of LGBTQIA+ Indians from the second century CE onwards, disproving any claims made about queer identities being antithetical to Indian culture, values, or traditions.

In this melded space, I find comfort in the acceptance and celebration of my queerness by my sister and my closest friends in Bombay. Over time, I built up the courage to come out to my parents who, while finding it difficult to accept, chose to prioritise my happiness above the dictates of society. I give gratitude for the validation of my identity and my choices by them, irrespective of their reservations and concerns. Here, I dream of the future in which my partner steps off a plane in Bombay and we rediscover that city together so that I might see it with new eyes and find happiness in it again, even if it will always be tinged by what has been lost. Here, I am learning to allow my contradictions to melt away so that I can become whole again, proudly owning the queerness of my Wendian self.

# Mother of Three Lovely Sons

## Jennifer

Dear Reader,

Imagine you were born in Namibia, a country in southwest Africa. Namibia is neighbours with South Africa, Botswana, Angola, and Zambia. Namibia is a beautiful country with a deep history, many beautiful sights to see, lives to lead, traditions to learn and follow, honour to uphold, and codes to live by. There is a verse of the Bible that talks about dead flies causing good perfume to stink. Similarly, bad practices that people turn a blind eye towards, end up ruining the good aspects of societies. It is because of this permitted evil that you run away from home.

Imagine being raped by your brother, your mother's son – not a half or stepbrother, but the one who occupied your mother's womb before you. Imagine you live in his house only because he is your brother, and your siblings support each other. Imagine that he violates you without remorse, without shame and consequence. Imagine he beats you while at it, because why would you resist? He is the man of the house; he has a right to everything – living and non-living – in the house, including you and your body. Imagine that he sanctions anyone that comes close to that body. It does not matter who or what you desire; he is the man of the house, and he can do as he likes.

Imagine now that you summon the courage and take the matter to the traditional council to report that your brother, who suckled the same breast you did, has now started, forcibly, sucking your breasts. They tell you they have heard, and they sympathise with

27

you. Sorry, they say – but he is the man of the house, and his actions, though wrong, cannot be penalised as he is the head of the family as per tradition. There is not much they can do. They advise you to run far away from home, to go as far as possible from him to a place where he cannot find you. You think that they are crazy. They admit that there has been wrongdoing but will not rise to do anything about it because your big brother is the traditional head of the family. You wonder if the same thing happens in their families, and they give the same pathetic excuse. Perhaps, their acknowledgement is only lip service, or maybe they are just spineless. You are angry because you are the one who is being violated, and you are the one who is being told to disappear. You do not bother to go to the police; they will not help either.

You had a man once; you loved him. You made a baby together – a boy. But it did not quite work out. You did not want the same things and he left. Then you met another man, and you loved each other. Your love was beautiful while in bloom. You made another baby – another boy – and he was ready to stay and be a father to his child and your older child. But your brother chased him away. Your brother wanted you to himself.

You are a woman in a country where there is no help forthcoming. You do what you can to make ends meet, but you have two mouths to feed, and what you make is never enough. So, when someone offers you a job in Turkey (they would arrange your visa and purchase your ticket), you take the opportunity and try to make a life for yourself and your children. You take your first child to your mother while your brother snatches the second one, who is only around two years old, from you. You did not stay back to fight because you know that is what he wants, and you will not win. You leave the child in his hands and run to the airport in Windhoek and fly to Turkey.

Welcome to Turkey. You get to Istanbul, and the welcome is not what you expected. There is no office to get to, no shop to man, nothing. They tell you the job starts soon, but you would be trained first. When your training begins, you realise you have been brought to this strange country to become a sex worker – a prostitute. You are expected to sleep with whoever they send you. You understand that you have actually been trafficked for sex. You are not alone; there are others.

You get together with one woman from your home country, Namibia and you run. You get to the airport in Istanbul, and while you are trying to find your way onto a flight, the traffickers catch you and take you back. They threaten you, watch you like hawks and keep trying to make a prostitute out of you. But you run again, and they catch you once more.

You did not escape incestuous rape in Namibia to become a prostitute in a country straddling Europe and Asia. So, once again, you run. This time, you do not run to the airport. You run to the closest Western Union office you can find because you know they would speak English. You explain your plight and ask for their help. They, too, cannot help you. So once again, you are asked to run. They tell you of a place called Antalya. It is far away, has an airport, and you would be long gone before they look for you there. So, they send you on your way with their best wishes and prayers.

There are many ways to get to Antalya from Istanbul. You could go by air, train or bus. You could not go to the airport because you would be caught again. You do not have the time and the presence of mind to go to the train station. So, you get on a bus and make the journey to Antalya.

The trip to Antalya is seventeen hours by road, but you do not know that when you set out. You simply hope and pray that they are not looking for you already and that they do not think of the bus station straight away if they are already looking for you. There must have been an immanent spirit watching over you because your prayers get answered and you are soon on your way. You are thankful to this immanent spirit, whatever he or she may be, for ensuring your escape this time, after three failed attempts.

The road to Antalya is long. You pass through all sorts of terrains on your way. You see beautiful plains, rolling hills and many, many stretches of land. As you make it to the Anatolian plateau, you start to think that this could be an enjoyable journey if you were not so anxious or running away. If you had a camera, you would have taken a video of the scenery and found a way to overlay it with a song about freedom. However, as you reach the southern part of the Anatolian plateau, you come across the Taurus mountains. The road becomes snakelike, winding its way through the mountains, bending and twisting around deep gorges and steep inclines. You realise that any miscalculation by the driver could result in your death. Indeed, anyone who does not have mastery over the terrain would definitely die. Even though the road is in good condition, the terrain is unrelenting. Your anxiety, which had almost turned to admiration because of the scenery of the earlier parts of the journey, turns to panic. Interestingly, it is your children that you worry about. What will become of your boys without their mother? What kind of men would they become without a guiding hand to show them the truth? Would they be cared for? Would your brother take revenge on them because you absconded? Would he force them to rape girls or carry drugs? You also think of yourself. Could you have come to this point only to die? If you die here, who would know? How would the news get home? Your mother, you are sure, would die of a broken heart. The certainty of death is much, much better than the uncertainty of being reported missing. You pray. You ask the immanent spirit to consider the torments you have undergone in the past and grant you this one wish – that you do not die in this strange terrain. You also ask the spirit to let you see your children again. Eventually, you make it to the light. After almost 400 kilometres of road across varied terrain, you make it to Antalya and head straight to the airport where you buy a plane ticket for a UK-bound flight. You hold your breath as you are checked in, looking around to see if any of the members of the prostitution and drugs ring are around. When your plane takes off, you exhale.

You start asking for a police officer the minute you land in the UK. Perhaps, everyone is surprised. When a youngish official-looking man comes to you, you do not trust him. All the people who have done you wrong, and made you run away from home into the hands of sex traffickers, and now into this new country to seek help, are men. So, you do not trust this youngish man without proof of who he says he is. The officer shows you a badge; you are satisfied and you tell your story. The officer listens to your story keenly; when you are done, he says you need help and takes you to immigration. At the immigration place, they ask you for your story and you tell them. They ask you for further details of your life and story, and you tell them what happened to the best of your knowledge. As you speak, they tap-tap on their computers and some of them even write things down. After this consultation, you are processed into the UK as an asylum seeker. You are safe.

Life in the UK is, to you, pretty straightforward. Having been granted asylum, you receive a stipend from the government for a while, but as a mother and an honourable woman, you know you have to work. As you see it, things are pretty straightforward – you work hard, you get paid; you use the money to improve yourself and care for your family back home. So, you get a job in a care home, and you work hard every day. You love your job because it pays the bills, but there is more. You love your job because you feel fulfilled taking care of old folks; it is as though you are caring for your grandparents. You hope that one day you will have enough money to open a care home too, so that you can take care of your mother and soothe her many aches.

Your mother – Mama – is the one true love of your life; she is your rock. She is the one caring for your two children now. She is the one who wrestled your second child from your evil brother when you ran away. She has taken care of both boys since then. Recently, your mother and the boys have moved to a hotel to protect her grandsons from your brother. Your mother has had to take special care since word got out about where you are and that you

31

are trying to get them to come to the UK. There is no telling what goes on in the mind of a spiteful man. He could harm the children somehow; he could kidnap or use them to push drugs. He could do anything to prevent you from gaining that freedom you desire and which you have worked so hard to achieve.

Back to life in the UK. Life in the UK has been eventful. As you settle down to work and live, you meet a man who reminds you of your second son's father. You hit it off, become friends and then lovers. Your relationship produces a son. But this man does not stay with you. Indeed, he has nothing to offer you besides his resemblance to a man you once loved and lost. He makes silly excuses, and you let him go. You keep the child like you have done twice before.

Things are getting better now. You have been to the African Community Centre in Swansea, where you live and work, and have learnt English as a second language. You also attend Gower College to improve your English language. The English language they speak here in Swansea is not like you speak in Namibia. Here in Swansea, they speak the real thing, and to learn this, you have to unlearn everything you imbibed before.

Things are good now. You find community in Swansea. You attend counselling, where you pour your heart out to the people who help you. As they speak with you, you start to speak to yourself. You have come this far from incest, rape, traffickers, prostitution, and the uncertainty of mountains, and you are here now. So, on bad days, when memory gets the better of you, you remind yourself what you have endured and overcome. You picture yourself and remind yourself that it is not the end yet. Your children and mother are still unsafe in Namibia, and you are doing everything possible to get them out of there. So, you start to speak to people privately, offering them hope and telling them that it cannot always be night. You ask them to find strength and light within themselves till the day breaks and a helping hand is sent their way. Not long after that, you get the chance to speak publicly. So, you use your story to inform and inspire others. You pour yourself into these talks and become a symbol of hope for many.

Things are good now, but every silver lining has an accompanying cloud. Sometimes, when you sleep at night, you wake up with a start thinking you hear your children calling you in the sitting room. You rise and go there; then you remember they are not yet with you. But a silver lining is a silver lining. Your children have got their visas; you are working on getting their tickets. You pray that you keep them hidden away long enough so your brother does not find them and foil well-laid plans. You know one day they will come, and you will be one family again. You will then feel complete – a mother of three lovely sons. You cannot wait for your older children to meet their newest brother. You just cannot wait.

If anyone asks you what your dreams are for the future, you tell them your vision is to give your children a better life, peace, education, and freedom to be. You dream that your boys will never be the kind of men who would force themselves on women who do not want them. You do not just dream this but rather, know that you will ensure this.

When pressed further, however, about your dreams for yourself – apart from your children – you tell them that you are planning to take a government-sponsored course so that you can get into business and make some more money to better your life and take care of loved ones. You tell them that you want a man who would love you and your boys and do right by you. You want a man who would, as Beyoncé says, put a ring on it. You have been alone for far too long, and you want a kind and loving man to protect you and your three lovely sons and be the man of the house in the way a man should be. You want to be whole.

Dear reader, do not imagine this story. Believe it. This is the life that I have lived; it is the life I still live.

Yours surviving,
Jennifer

# Home

## Chandrika Joshi

I was fourteen when I left the country of my birth, Uganda, and came to live in Wales. My father, a Hindu priest, had moved to Uganda from India in 1935. In 1945 my father had returned to India, to get married and soon after my mother joined him in Uganda, and they started a family. They returned to India to seek medical help in 1952 for their first born, who didn't survive. My siblings and I were born in Uganda and we thought Uganda was our home. For my parents it was different. They were aware of the political climate with the policy of Africanisation in East Africa. When Kenya expelled Asians in 1968, my parents were forced to make an investigative trip to India, in the fear of being kicked out of Uganda.

In August 1972, Idi Amin Dada, the president of Uganda gave ninety days' notice to 80,000 Asians to leave Uganda. When the announcement took place, my sister Madhu, and I were living in a girls hostel in Kampala in order for us to study at Kololo Senior Secondary School, one of the best secondary schools in Uganda. My older brother Pankaj was studying for his A levels at a Grammar school in Birmingham. Education was the most important thing, for my parents, who were not given that chance when they were children. They were adamant that they would do their utmost to educate all their children. In a country where education was not free, I knew I was privileged because my parents could afford to pay my school fees. I was in my second year of secondary school and Madhu was in her final year and was due to take her O level exams in December 1972.

Once Amin gave his notice, our lives started unravelling. My sister and I were sent back home from our school. Our school knew we would not be returning and handed us our final reports to be given to our future schools. When we returned to our little village, Iganga, it was in turmoil. People had their eyes fixed on the *Uganda Argus* (the daily print newspaper published in Kampala), and their ears tuned to the radio – hoping that Amin would announce that it was a joke and he had changed his mind. The atmosphere in the town turned ominous and eerie. There were army personnel in the village, and we were warned not to go out in the evenings. We heard the grownups talking about beatings and killings. One day out of the blue, our home help John, didn't show up for work. In fact, he didn't come for many days and when he returned, he told us that he had been locked up by the police. He showed us his bare back, full of long, thin wounds at various stages of healing. His jailers wanted him to tell them which Asian family had employed him. John was a shy young man and looking back, I even think he had a mild learning disability. Despite the beatings, he did not tell his captors about us. We were exceedingly grateful to him.

Everyone in our town was making vital decisions of their lives – whether to stay despite Amin's warning, or to flee; and if the latter, where to? My aunt had a home in India. She had only come to Uganda to help my mother take care of us, children, when my father sustained a stroke in 1965. My mother came from a happy, loving family and had her siblings in India, so my aunt and mother wanted to return to India. My father had been orphaned as a child and knew how tough life could be in India, and would not budge. He insisted on us going to the UK. Besides, he did not want to split the family as my brother was already in a boarding school in Birmingham.

Asian people believe in 'strength in numbers', and consider having relatives a huge advantage in life. Many people we knew had relatives in the UK, and they were able to plan ahead for themselves, as they felt secure in the knowledge that someone would show them the ropes once they emigrated. We were at a disadvantage as my parents

36

were the only members of their family who lived in Uganda, and we had no one in the UK to fall back on. Additionally, illness had rendered my father disabled and that also was a disadvantage for us. The Ugandan army had set up checkpoints on main roads leading to Kampala and Entebbe (where the airport was). The Asians who travelled on these roads were searched, and anything valuable was confiscated by army personnel – this included money which they were carrying to buy flight tickets. When my father had gone to Kampala to buy the flight tickets, my mother and aunt had prayed and waited with bated breath.

Our family exploded with excitement when my father returned with our tickets. We were flying in two days' time (on 13 October), on a British Caledonian flight to London, Heathrow. Every person with a valid ticket could carry twenty kilos of luggage and my father could take £50 worth of cash. After working hard in Uganda for thirty-seven years, my father was left with little more than what he had when he started out. Also, he was no longer alone – he had a wife and six children to look after. My parents bought eight blue suitcases, and we were given white emulsion paint to write our names on the suitcases. My younger brother Atul, and I busied ourselves writing names of family members whilst we chatted about our upcoming flight. We were all asked to put our favourite toys and other items in our cases by my mother. On the day of our flight, taxis came to take us away. Before we left, we went to John and told him we were leaving, and that he could take anything he liked from our home. John gingerly came into the house and stood before the pile of ironed clothes looking confused and overwhelmed. Meanwhile, another home help we used to have, called Okwire, had brought his friends who started moving the furniture out. We never found out whether John ever managed to take away the ironed clothes.

I have no memory of landing at Heathrow airport but remember travelling by coach to a train station. As I watched the English villages the coach went through, thoughts of Enid Blyton's books that I had read at school came to my mind. We boarded our train which, after many hours, brought us to a remote, windy train-station called Tonfanau. It was a cold evening and I recall my teeth chattering. We had come to a country I had never heard of – Wales. We had arrived in Tonfanau, an abandoned army barracks near Tywyn in Meirionnydd district in Gwynedd. This was to be our temporary home in Wales. This was the resettlement camp for Ugandan Asians.

As soon as we were allocated our huts, we went straight to bed. The next morning, I looked outside our window and stared. I asked myself where all the colour had disappeared to, as everything outside seemed to be soaked in cold, muted grey. I was sure I went to sleep with colours behind my eyes but now they had all faded away and were replaced with various shades of grey. I have a photograph of me smiling, in my favourite blue dress and my brown strapped sandals, surrounded by the teachers and students of our temporary school at the camp, and I wonder if the smile on that girl's face was painted on a mask. The person that I am, and that was the real me, was buried inside that girl's heart. She did come out every once in a while, and then the girl in the blue dress had a panic attack and could not stop shaking. We collected our blue suitcases from one of the offices after a breakfast of toast and tea at a communal canteen not far from our hut.

'We need to contact Pankaj straight away'; my parents asked my sister and I to try and phone my brother. My sister and I had never used a public telephone. After asking around, we went to the iconic red telephone box opposite the Globe Cinema to figure out how to use it. We ran back to our hut and collected fifty pence worth of two pence coins and stuffed our skinny bodies in the red booth again, and dialled the number of my brother's college. We told the person who answered the phone at the other end, to inform my brother that we were safe and that we were staying in a camp in Wales.

'Where in Wales?' the man asked;

'What's the name of this place? I asked my sister.

She pointed to the label which said TYWYN.

I looked at the word and faltered. How on earth do I pronounce this word? I thought to myself. All I could do was spell it out. In and amongst everything else, this was also my introduction to the Welsh language.

Pankaj was unrecognisable when he came to see us that weekend. I had last seen him nearly two years earlier, just before I started secondary school. He had been seventeen then and I was twelve. After coming to the UK he had adopted the classic 1970s look, sideburns and all. He was my oldest brother, and I thought the world of him. He had brought me a gift – a little blue tartan handbag. What he had not realised, was that the bag he had bought was a child's bag and I was no longer a child.

A month down the line, my aunt's relatives visited us from London. We had sent multiple parcels to their addresses and they had made a trip to unite us with our worldly goods. The boxes, still covered in red and green fabric sewn together tightly, contained my father's books and our kitchen utensils and spices. As soon as we were able to cook our own food, these spices came in handy.

My sister was given a place at Dolgellau Grammar School, so that she could sit her O levels that she had been due to sit in Uganda with the Cambridge board. In December of 1972, I too got selected to go to Tywyn Grammar School with a handful of other people from the camp. I soon struck up a firm friendship with another girl from the camp and we hung out together most of the time at school. I was, however, desperate to make Welsh friends. I wondered what their houses were like from the inside, what games they played, what they talked about when they chattered in groups. There was one Welsh girl, who was very friendly and when I ran after her, in desperation, wanting to be her friend, I was chastised by my friend from the camp. In mid-December, we sat our first exams and topped the class.

On 8 February 1973, we were taken to Penrhys in the Rhondda

to our new council house. Penrhys was like a hillfort – with a mound of houses and flats in the centre of the estate and a circular road called Heol Pendyrus encircling the estate like a trench. At the entrance of the village there is an ancient shrine to St Mary. This place has been a place of pilgrimage for the Catholic people despite the destruction of the original statue during the Reformation.

The day we arrived in Penrhys coincided with the Hindu festival of *Vasant Panchami*, to mark the beginning of spring. It is similar to *Imbolc*, the Gaelic festival, which is dedicated to St Brigid. *Vasant Panchami* is associated with the goddess Saraswati, the water goddess of wisdom, arts, and music. The colour associated with this festival is yellow, the colour of sunshine, the colour of daffodils. The colours that had been absent in the camp, returned. My life was no longer in black and white.

Our house was on the highest point of the estate, a grey, mid-terrace property, squeezed between the houses that belonged to Jean and Joanna. They later became friends with my mother and aunt and their children befriended my youngest siblings. When we arrived at the location, a woman from Rhondda Borough Council was waiting for us at the door. We opened the gate and entered a small courtyard surrounded by a high wooden fence. At the end of the courtyard was a three-bedroom house with a kitchen, upstairs bathroom, and a sitting room. The furniture in the house was minimal and shabby, but we were very happy to finally have somewhere to unload our large blue suitcases and call home.

That week, an education officer visited us in order to allocate schools for us. While my younger siblings and older sister were allocated the primary school and Grammar school respectively, my brother and I were appointed to the Ferndale secondary modern school. I asked to be sent to the Grammar school instead and my request was accepted. I wondered why I had not made the same request for my brother at the time, and have lived with the guilt ever since. My brother, while bright with good grades from Uganda, saw his school days as a waste of time. His academic potential was unfortunately not fully realised. At the time, the fact that we, in Uganda, had received a good level of education, similar to the British curriculum, was not recognised.

From the very first day, the learning curve was a steep one for me, more culturally than academically. Initially, my style of dressing was outdated and not trendy. I had grown up mostly listening to Bollywood music and was unaware of almost all of the popular pop stars and magazines that the girls my age were following and pouring over. My classmates, while asking me questions about my life in Africa, also began educating me in all the trends, although, smoking at the age of fourteen in the girls' toilets was a habit that shocked me at the time and so did swearing and disrespecting teachers. Those first few years, I struggled with the loss of my culture and not having any Indian friends but once I settled, I developed deep friendships with Welsh people and began integrating into my new surroundings, life, and culture, while still retaining our Ugandan/Indian culture.

It has now been over fifty years since a fourteen-year-old girl first stepped off a train in Wales and while my memories of my childhood in Uganda remain, Wales has been my home for most of my life. It has been a rollercoaster ride at times, where I have gained a lot, but have also lost a lot. At times, I have gone through life with pangs of *hiraeth* in my heart – a longing for home, even though now, Wales is the closest thing to home that I could ever envisage.

# The Many Roads to Becoming:
# A Journey from Pakistan to Wales

## A.E. Gill

I look back at my seventeen-year-old self in 1997, bubbling with imagination, ambitions, and dreams, especially the dream to be highly educated. At the age when most of my peers were merely interested in trying new beauty tips, I was trying my utmost to find opportunities to educate myself. Towards this end, I used to read every bit of paper that I could lay my hands upon, be it newspapers or a paper wrapped around something my mother bought from the market. I would hastily unwrap and read through it. Sometimes my obsession with reading made my father worry about me, and he used to scold me and ask me to pay more attention to household chores rather than reading, since this is what good girls are expected to do. It was both my pleasure and obsession; the curiosity to discover new things, places, people, and pose unending questions to the supposed all-knowing adults around me. But my logical reasoning used to come against illogical answers to questions such as, 'Aren't those who study also "good girls"?'

I am the oldest daughter of the family and it was very hard for my parents to put me through school. However, they did so by working very hard. Both my parents would work to earn the family's bread and butter, and I would work at home to ensure that the domestic machinery functioned smoothly by looking after my younger brothers and sisters. I always dreamed of being a son for my parents since a male child is thought to be an earning and dependable hand for parents in Third World societies. My dreams were not to follow the normal social norms, but to stand out by getting a good education and then enable my parents to educate my siblings to a higher level. I had concluded at an early age, education was the surest way to the top. My parents enrolled all of us not only in the local school, but also in Church activities in conjunction with religious education at home. They passed on to us the legacy of being thankful for whatever little we had.

In 1999 my parents, following the cultural traditions and pressure, arranged my marriage and I became a wife to a man I barely knew, irrespective of the fact that I had young responsible men in my life who I admired and who could have made far better life partners. I obediently settled for the choice that was made for me, in the hope that somewhere along the journey, love would fill the holes dug by fear, doubt, and uncertainty. In our culture a girl has no say in whether or not she wants to get married. Moreover, Christians being very few in number in Pakistan, are always forced to go with the social flow of the Muslim norms. Cutting a long story short, I got married with a heart full of pain for my shattered dreams. My dream of attaining a higher education, my ultimate wish to earn money and be a helping hand for my parents and siblings, and establishing a school for girls from the Christian community, all took a back seat. Pleasing my husband and in-laws became the first priority of my life.

I started trying to make my husband a priority, from the kitchen, to the bedroom, to bearing his children and servicing the myriad expectations of in-laws in a joint family system. In obedience to his commands, I started avoiding my parents and limited my contact with them despite living in the same city. But despite my efforts to comply, I was still subjected to brutal beatings, the worst of which came for reading books. My husband was very suspicious about what I read and looked for in the world of print. Our thinking patterns were as apart as the earth and sky. He was of the view that books spoil and corrupt women, making them stubborn and uncontrollable.

Amid all this turmoil, I gave birth to my first child and thought it might be a sign of divine intervention that could improve the fortunes of my young marriage. I thought the spark of newness, new life and an additional human to protect, would soften my husband's brutish behaviour. But all my hopes went down the drain when I realised that giving birth to a baby girl is little less than the most heinous crime. My husband blamed me and said that the child was not his, as in their family the firstborn is always a male child. As he questioned my character, I could not remain calm and spoke out to clear my name. Yet nothing resolved the situation, and on top of it, my husband's violent behaviour and mental torture on account of his doubting nature added to my misery. My second child was a boy, but I still regret that my daughter has no good memory associated with her father.

This was the story of my early marital years, which made me realise how badly I was confined and entangled in a horrific bond. If I ever tried to speak to someone about the situation, he threatened me with physical torture and also threatened me by saying that he would gamble over me. The situation got so intolerable that I had to share it with my parents. When he found this out, he tried to set me ablaze. This was the most terrifying moment. I felt my life slip through my body, and as I ran I thought of my children and wondered who would love them like I did. I thought of all my dreams, which I had still hoped would come to fruition someday. I barely escaped being totally burnt, as I was saved in time, but the incident left scars not only on my body, but also on my soul. My father suffered a heart attack when he heard the news, and soon he was fighting for his life in hospital, while I was helpless, not knowing what to do. I felt defeated and my hopes of my marriage being redeemed by a sheer miracle or intervention of nature, were dashed.

After this, I resolved to live like an entirely numb person, unfeeling, devoid of dreams and with zero expectations. I sealed my lips and mentally prepared myself for, and accepted whatever torture was hurled my way. The physical and mental abuse continued for years. Being violated by a man I called my husband became second nature, and torture became a norm and a constant. I always knew what was sure to follow at the slightest altercation. Then one day, I was shaken up and was brought to my senses when he, under a high dose of narcotics, attacked my daughter and pierced her hand with sharp scissors. The running blood of my innocent child and the savage behaviour of her father challenged my motherhood, and the raw instinctive power to protect my child burst to the surface. That very night I escaped with my two children from there and sought refuge at my parents' home. But we were not safe there so we kept moving for a short period in order to hide away from him.

During that time, he subjected my parents, brother, and sisters to many brutal beatings so as to find out my whereabouts. He stopped at nothing and fully made use of the influence of his underworld and political connections. We could not put a stop to his wrath and brutality. It went to the extent where he kidnapped my daughter from school and sold her, while gambling for a few rupees and drugs. I rescued my daughter with the help of my brother, but she was so terrified that she sank into silence and stopped going to school. Then my parents proposed that I move to another country where my, and my children's rights could be protected and we could lead a safe life. They helped me arrange funds and after a few years' struggle, I came to the UK.

I came to the UK with two of my children, but my youngest son is still in Pakistan. He has been sold to my sister-in-law in exchange for a few rupees by my husband.

Life brought me to the UK on 20 December 2012 along with my two children, when I had nothing to rely on apart from the protection of my God. It was my first international journey and I could not speak English. I came here as a shattered, battered woman, bereaved of all her hopes. Starting from scratch was not easy, but I knew there was no easy path leading to success. The only saving grace was the feeling of being in a safe place where humans are treated like humans, far away from the shadows of an abusive and unfeeling husband and father. I held on to God's promise that He would lead me into my 'promised land' and I was ready to follow Him. Faith became an opium, a soothing escape from unsavoury realities. I held onto my unwavering faith and jittery hopes like a drowning man to the last straw.

Soon, our journeys to multiple unknown and unplanned destinations began. The thing about claiming asylum in the United Kingdom is that you become a government entity. This implies that you could be moved to several destinations without having any say on where, when or how these destinations are allocated. You only travel light and never acquire more than you can carry, as the moving van will only move you once and you can only take what the van can accommodate. A minimalist approach to life became a virtue. Birmingham was the first city we were placed in, followed by London, Cardiff, and finally Swansea, which has been a home to me and my children for the last twelve years. It was the first time in years that we could sleep in peace and go about life without fear and with less anxiety. My children were excited to join the school, and when they were in school, I was a prisoner of solitude, left with depression and migraines. I would pace around the house, anxious and paranoid, brooding on past events and humbled by not knowing what would come next. The uncertainty of not having a major source of income, even while being capable of performing in the capacity of a midwife, a skill I acquired while in Pakistan, deflated my confidence. Once we gave up our passports at the airport, we also gave up our identity and embraced uncertainty. The state of never knowing what happens next, and where we will be moved next, made us free fugitives; we had escaped our household demons but had taken refuge in a home far away from home with its new demons. But of the two 'evils', this was a lesser one, less likely to draw blood. The government monthly stipend was helpful but insufficient. I had so many intrinsic issues to deal with and the refusals from the Home Office were adding fuel to the fire of anxiety of another kind. I was neither in control of my life nor that of the little lives I brought with me. But as the Lord is never too early, never too late but always on time, I met a nurse just when I needed it most. She referred me to the African Community Centre and advised me to take a few counselling sessions. This marked the beginning of my journey towards getting help, opening up and embracing therapy.

At first, I could hardly muster up the courage to go there as my poor language skills and rock-bottom confidence levels deterred me. But I was so pleased to make that decision of going there as it brought me in contact with Jill, a wonderful counsellor who opened windows to invite the light back into my dark mind through the first counselling session. I had been in such a vulnerable state of mind, and it was hard to trust anyone. For the early sessions, I was mute, partly from lack of trust, poor expression and then confusion of not knowing what to say and where to start. I could not respond to anything, though it felt exhilarating, just sitting and staring into thin space. Over time, Jill won my trust by making confidentiality the highest of her priorities about our counselling sessions. I started taking my children to a local church and in a few months' time, the ACC's manager asked me to join sewing classes. I joined the classes and the feeling was great, as I felt useful in staying part of something productive, an impactful project at that, instead of sitting at home gazing at moving vehicles and people, or lost in thought.

At some point, our sewing teacher had to undergo surgery. The manager asked me if I was well-versed in sewing. I said that I could just about manage. Thereafter, she asked me to take over the teaching for the sewing class. This opened a lot of opportunities for me as ACC started sending me to represent them in different training sessions and seminars. Life took a major turn towards calm and normality. The ACC and the Oxfam Livelihood Project, helped me to discover myself and brought the best out of me. It was as though this project awakened and ushered in a new me. I started picking up the threads of my dreams again which I once had abandoned. Life became an intricate yarn moving in and out through the eye of a needle. I painted my dreams in colour; a spectrum of sartorially appealing couture.

Today, I am not in a competition with anyone, nor am I trying to overshadow someone else's achievements. I am just striving to be a better person than what I was yesterday. I am a peer-mentor today and God has enabled me to help many other time-battered women like the one I once was. Now, my children are getting the world's best education and becoming a part of such a thriving society far away from the violence of monsters in human form. I volunteer with Cancer Research for two days, translate and interpret with ACC during counselling sessions, study ESOL at Entry 3 level, actively participate in church activities and above all, I find peace and joy doing all this. My daughter has now married the love of her life and given me grandchildren. My son is working while studying for a higher degree.

I see myself in my granddaughter – vivacious, full of zest for life, and quite energetic. But I feel so much peace knowing that the road to her becoming will not be as hard as the many paths I took with my children towards securing our identity. There are still struggles but the worst is over. There is a part of this journey that I can never find the right expression to narrate. I was alone, raising my children for twelve years. During those twelve years, I felt cold, but I was also alone and lonely. I yearned for some masculine support, a father figure for my fast-growing children. I would tuck my children in and sing them to sleep and then hug my pillow in the vain hope that it would banish all the cold and loneliness I felt. For twelve years, I did not feel the touch of a man; I did not feel the warmth and satisfaction of companionship. I suppressed all desires of the flesh and perished the idea of ever being with a man. I felt almost claustrophobic and would gasp for breath whenever I found myself in the midst of too many men. I had mental flashes of my children's father, dragging me across the cold wet floors of our home in Pakistan, screaming and pulling me with trails of blood in his wake. The ghosts of my past formed shadows in my memory and flashed before my eyes as soon as any man as much as made the slightest advances towards me. Trust is a currency that once broken, may never be regained easily.

I currently work as an Admin Officer in a project that caters to the management of mental and emotional wellbeing. As the former Chairperson of the Swansea City of Sanctuary, I established strong connections with Wales and volunteered in diverse capacities especially with the City Church in Swansea. I decided to settle in Wales as I had formed firm bonds of friendship with Welsh friends, and I now regard Wales as home. Having said that, I also recall, that when I first arrived in Wales, I was always lonely until I gradually began to integrate and learn English. Language had been a major barrier for me when I arrived here. But through the support of the City of Sanctuary, I began to thrive and have even managed to gain influence across groups in the third sector.

I wish to adopt counselling as a profession in future and wish to participate in projects for girls' health and education. In the end I want to show my gratitude for God's blessings which have reached me through Oxfam, ACC, my Church, and also the Border Agency who have facilitated us to start a new life. My heart is full of gratitude for the journey covered and the many paths taken to our destination today. With the receipt of our Leave-To-Remain, there are so many more opportunities at our disposal. My life is a testimony, a dream I keep waking up from, every single day.

# Finding Bollywood in Friog

## Mohini Gupta and Noorie

### Celebrating Diwali in Wales

It was a cold November in Aberystwyth, and I was homesick. This happened a day before Diwali in 2017. I usually pride myself on being independent and detached from name, place, animals, and things, but this festival of lights always makes me nostalgic for home and family in a way that is completely inexplicable.

The thought of home for me, is tied intricately to food. The only cure for homesickness in my understanding is food. It can transport you back in time to people, to places, to memory. I had tried many restaurants in and around Aberystwyth to satiate this irrational search for food, which would help manage the nostalgia I felt, but had been disappointed on every occasion.

When I mentioned that it was Diwali, and that I was dying to eat 'authentic' Indian food to my friend Catrin, she offered to drive me to a restaurant which was up the coast from Aberystwyth, a place that she thought might be authentic. Now, I trust Catrin's taste in food, so I took a leave of absence for the day from my Welsh tutor and decided to take this leap of faith.

After a long and winding drive up to Fairbourne, we arrived at this restaurant called 'Indiana cuisine'. Imagine my surprise when I walked in and bumped into a familiar looking face from Bollywood – our host for the evening and the owner of the said restaurant. He was as delighted to see me, another Indian, especially someone who recognised him immediately in these remote parts, and ended up sharing his *Yaadon-Ki-Baarat* (a procession of memories) photo album with me. There were pictures of him with famous Bollywood celebrities including the likes of Shahrukh Khan, Salman Khan, Sanjay Dutt; it even included letters that some of them had written to him. He talked at length about his 'mama', as maternal uncles are called in India, and it was only later I realised that he was talking about the Marlon Brando of Indian cinema – Amitabh Bachchan. It may not be an apt comparison, but I cannot think of another Western icon who could represent what Bachchan means to Indian cinema. I had always known the actor-restauranteur by his screen name, 'Master Mayur'. He was well-known in India for having portrayed the young Bachchan in some of his most celebrated movies like *Deewar* and *Namak Halal*. It was only now that I found out that his real name was Raj – the ultimate romantic name for connoisseurs of Hindi cinema. His wife Noorie was the *chef de cuisine*.

Needless to say, the food at the restaurant was as 'authentic' as I needed it to be on this day. We started with a portion of poppadoms and delicious chutneys, followed by some excellent Seekh Kababs and a serving of Fish Amritsari. The main course included the most delectable Indian dishes I have eaten outside of India – from the melt-in-the-mouth Coconut Lamb Curry to the uniquely piquant Methi Chicken. The Jeera Aloo and Bhindi Do Pyaza brought back memories of school tiffins packed with love, and the garlic naans were baked to perfection. The next time I went to Indiana Cuisine, I took the scenic train ride along the coastline from Aberystwyth to Pwllheli with a group of fifteen Welsh friends, who simply loved the experience. Soon I became a familiar face at Indiana Cuisine. Raj told me that their children were attending Welsh-medium schools. I was surprised that this Indian couple had chosen to settle down in Dolgellau of all places in the UK.

## Cross-cultural journeys

Historically, India and Wales share many interesting connections. The Welsh missionaries had a deep impact on the north-east region of India, and even contributed to establishing some languages as written languages for the first time ever. It is for this reason that the *Khasi* community, an ethnic group of over 1.5 million people concentrated in the state of Meghalaya, still sing their anthem to the tune of the Welsh National Anthem, 'Hen Wlad Fy Nhadau'. Schools that were started by Welsh missionaries in different parts of India continued to hold a version of the Eisteddfod until very recently – an alumnus of St Mary's School, Pune, from 1967 reminisces about her school saying, 'There were fetes and fairs and socials at the Eisteddfod' (Vignettes Newsletter 2010). In fact, my mother went to the same school and participated in Eisteddfod competitions in the 1970s too.

I recently discovered the story of a young woman, Dorothy Bonarjee, who left India and moved to England with her family at the age of ten. She decided that she wanted to study French at the University College of Wales in Aberystwyth back in 1912, and became the first Asian woman to ever win a chair at the College Eisteddfod. Bonarjee was an exceptional poet, debater, and a dynamic student who made quite an impact in Aberystwyth, and later went on to become the first woman to gain an internal law degree from University College London. In an uncanny reprise of Bonarjee's journey, I arrived in Aberystwyth from New Delhi to write and translate poetry, on a fellowship sponsored by the Charles Wallace India Trust and Literature Across Frontiers, more than a hundred years later in 2017. I was selected to translate Vikram Seth's verse into Hindi and write a set of original poems for young readers in India. This fellowship gave me a chance to spend three months in Wales, but the deep connection I formed with the life, language, and literature of Aberystwyth continues to play a significant role in my life even today. The language politics of Wales seemed familiar to me as a student of language; the warmth of the people made me feel at home; the cadences of the Welsh language sounded intimately familiar to my Indo-Italian ear (my father grew up in Italy and we still have family there).

What I had never seen before were the gorgeous sunsets, the walks on the promenade, and the vibrant pubs and restaurants in a town that felt so terribly safe for women, so different from my experience of growing up in Delhi. I started learning the Welsh language to feel even more connected to the town and found that my knowledge of Hindi and Sanskrit aided my language learning immensely. The grammar and phonetics of the Welsh language seemed to mirror those of Sanskrit, and in fact, I used Sanskrit phonetics to understand *treiglad* in the Welsh language. 'Yn Bangor' changes to 'Ym Mangor' because 'b' and 'm' are both labial consonants in the Sanskrit language – they are spoken with the lips. Similarly, 'Yn Derwen' becomes 'Yn Nerwen' because both 'd' and 'n' are dental consonants in Sanskrit – they are pronounced using the teeth. All of the above, is to emphasise that there are deep-rooted connections within the Indo-European roots of both languages, and this only adds to the multiple connections between the two nations.

### The life of Noorie

During that brief sojourn in 2017 in Aberystwyth, I became friends with many people whose presence I continue to cherish in my life, and one of them is Faaeza Jasdanwalla-Williams, who had also made a similar journey to Aberystwyth from Mumbai in India, and had fallen in love with the town instantly. She has in fact made it her home, completing her PhD from the University of Aberystwyth, and settling down to teach there. She has won the Welsh learner of the year award; and met and married her husband, and lives with him in Aberystwyth. We shared our love for Wales and India, Welsh and Urdu, song and poetry, and of course, food. When Faaeza asked me to contribute to an anthology she was editing that was focused on women's stories of migration from Asia, Africa, and the Middle East to Wales; the first person who came to my mind was Noorie. I had been to Indiana Cuisine so many times by then, but had never had the chance to speak at length with the person who made the magic happen in the kitchen. That is when I reached out to Raj, who connected me with Noorie. We could not meet in person as I no longer lived in Wales, but Noorie and I managed to have lengthy conversations over the phone.

Noorie grew up in a town called Kapurthala in the state of Punjab, close to the famous Golden Temple at Amritsar. She was introduced to Raj through her aunt. By the time they met he had already made the UK his home. Raj had moved to the UK in 1992 to set up a TV channel, in collaboration with his 'mama', Amitabh Bachchan. In fact, his company TV Asia was the first Asian TV channel to be established in the UK. Raj used to travel frequently to Mumbai in those years. During one of his trips to India, he met Noorie in New Delhi and they decided to get married in 2001. Noorie moved to Mumbai after the wedding. Noorie and Raj lived in Mumbai, where Noorie worked as a teacher and Raj continued to work in the Hindi cinema industry, moving back and forth between Mumbai and the UK.

Noorie first came to Wales on holiday with her husband in 2002. They stayed in the village of Aberdyfi (Aberdovey) on the west coast and fell in love with the area. They found the people to be kind and generous and she immediately decided that they had to come back here. And in 2006, they finally did move to Wales. They chose Dolgellau, a place that felt warm and welcoming to them. They also spent time looking for schools for their two children, Aazaan and Suhaana, with facilities that would take care of them. Noorie says she enjoyed dropping them to school and picking them up, and taking them to the town centre.

'When we finally moved here, we realised we were missing our Indian food and culture. Everything was very beautiful, but also very Welsh. We wanted to add some masala. That's the reason we decided to open a small business to introduce the local people to authentic Indian food. We felt that food would be a perfect introduction to Indian culture,' recounts Noorie.

Noorie says that Friog (Fairbourne) was referred to as a 'dead town' as they were shortlisting homes for themselves, but they ended up visiting the place anyway when Raj was invited for the inauguration of the railway station. They thought it was an extremely 'cute seaside village' and had no idea that the universe would bring them back to this place. A friend of theirs, Rod, later spoke to them about the village at length and said it had potential. This is how they ended up opening their restaurant there within six months of moving to Wales, and ran it for years until they recently moved to Plas Talgarth near Machynlleth. Initially, Noorie would divide her time between working as a beautician in Abermawr (Barmouth) and working at their restaurant in Friog, until she started working there full-time. Her father was a well-known chef and her passion for cooking came from having watched him cook as a child.

I asked her why she chose to send her children to a Welsh-medium school when it seemed so much more difficult than gaining their education through the medium of English. 'We chose to send our kids to Dolgellau School, which was a Welsh-medium school called Ysgol Gynradd Dolgellau. And even though it was tough for them, we felt that it was very important that they learn Welsh as they have to live here and be a part of the community,' said Noorie. She confessed that it was a struggle for them to adjust in a Welsh school, but the language has been a window to a different world for them. They even sent their children to special classes, and in fact, Noorie attended these special classes too and found them interesting. Her children speak Welsh fluently now, whereas she still struggles.

'It was Raj's dream to live in North Wales,' she reminisces. When asked about her greatest achievement, she says, 'I feel very lucky that the people here respect me as a chef, and sometimes even if I do not recognise them, they know me by name!' I asked Noorie what the greatest obstacle was while adjusting to their life in Wales. She admits that while learning the language was one of the most challenging issues, the beauty and simplicity of Wales has held them in a thrall. As someone who continues to return to the country for the same reasons, I could not agree more. Even though I did not reside in Wales for more than three months in 2017, my bond with Wales, its people, and the language runs deep. Geographically, I might be currently residing in Oxford, but Wales is in my heart and I escape to visit it at every opportunity – and each time it feels like I am coming home, albeit another kind of home.

# Dreaming of Joy in Chaos

## Shana

I came to the UK after the COVID-19 pandemic with my husband and four children. We did not come to this country as asylum seekers, we were people of moderate means. I had stability in my country; stability meant I had a home, a thriving food business and a community of friends, support systems and associates. My husband and I, along with our children lived in peace. Algeria is surrounded by neighbouring countries full of rich culture and history. Morocco, our neighbour to the west, is a country full of bustling trade and culture, separated from Portugal by the Strait of Gibraltar. To the east, is the country of Libya, which has been at war for decades. Other countries like Niger and Mali with their French and Arabic histories surround us, bringing a beautiful diversity to our region. Algeria then was the place to be. I was happy there and enjoyed my life.

The world would always remember 2020. Like many other countries, Algeria was hit with COVID and was locked down. We were cut off from the filial relationships we once enjoyed. So, it was only natural that after the devastation of the deadly disease, my husband told me that he wanted us to go to the UK and visit family. It was not an outlandish idea; indeed, we had gone to the UK four times before.

We flew to the UK and I loved the feeling of looking down on London from above – the waterways, the bridge, and the general efficient planning of the city. I was also fascinated by the fact that underneath all that you saw from the sky, there was still an underground railway system that was even faster than the surface rail network. I therefore, enjoyed my trip to the UK, connecting with family and making the most of what the city had to offer for what I thought was, holidaymakers such as us. I stayed with my sister; we went shopping and took in the sites. It was as though I was coming to a place I had never been before. We oscillated between visiting with my family and visiting with my husband's family for about fifteen days and soon it was time to return to Algeria.

As I started preparing the family to return home, my husband told me that we could not return because he had problems in Algeria. Though I was shocked because I thought our life in Algeria was perfect, I listened as he told me the story of his suffering. I did not know any of this, because he had shielded me and the children from it all. But it seemed as if things had taken a dangerous turn, and the situation with which he was dealing, would no longer spare the family. Having listened to him, and weighed the situation, we decided that it was best to seek asylum.

The decision to seek asylum was not one we took lightly. Though we both had family in the UK, we could not just stay and freeload off them. Staying in the UK without the proper documentation would mean that our children could not go to good schools, or that my husband and I would have to look over our shoulders every time we were in a crowd, or panic every time we saw an officer of the law. There is nothing that erodes one's sense of self faster than being in a place where one is not wanted, while praying not to get caught.

So, to keep my family – especially the children – safe, we stopped our holidaying and went to the Home Office to apply for asylum. After our application, we were put on the list and were put up in a hotel with other asylum seekers. The first thing I experienced was shock. How could I, not fleeing war or devastation of any kind, and who had come to this country of my own free will, now become a refugee? How could I, who lived in my own home, and had stability and a business, now live off the government's generosity? How could the six of us – my husband, myself and four children – live in a single hotel room? Everything I anchored my personality on, vanished with that application. I was like a full-grown adult who had just been born. I had a new country, a new language, new life; and all this was not by choice.

I could not speak my native language because no one would understand me. I could not understand people when they spoke. Yet some things did not change. I still had my children to cater for. I still had a husband to love and attend to. I still had a past to remember. When you are an asylum seeker – especially one who has not been officially granted refugee status, the things that once gave you comfort could metamorphose into a burden. But I am a mother and a wife, and I would never regard my children as burdens, neither would I resent my husband for plunging us into this life. I would admit to one thing, however – those days were hard.

We resided in our government-issued hotel for one year and five months. Our one-room had a bathroom, and that was it. We were not allowed to cook. We had to eat what was provided. Usually, the food was cold and uninspiring. Frequently, we were given sandwiches. Sometimes, we had canned food that had been emptied out into plastic plates and microwaved. I remember asking about the plastic plates and the hazard that microwaving food in them could pose, and I was told that the plastic plates were specifically made for the microwave. My children had a lot of stomach aches during that period.

The government gave us £40 a week, which meant that my family received about £240 every week. Unfortunately, that money was only in theory. In practice, from the money that the government released, we only received £8 individually. The cost of our food and some other essentials would have been taken out of the initial £40 amount promised to us. Likes and dislikes did not come into the equation, especially where food was concerned. What mattered was that we ate what was given to us, or the alternative was to make our own way, or starve. We certainly could not make our own way, since we were neither allowed to work nor cook for ourselves, so we had no choice.

Prior to being given accommodation in the hotel where we spent almost a year and a half, we had to spend one night in a police station on account of not finding a place to stay. The government had refused our application for accommodation at the time, so we went to the police station to seek help. My youngest child, who had never entered a police station before, urinated on herself because of fear and shock. I could understand that shock completely – one minute we were happy holidaymakers preparing to return to our country, and the next minute our life had turned upside down, and we were in the police station asking for help in order to not be sent back home. From then on, throughout our time in London, she suffered from stress-induced urinary incontinence.

In fact, she has suffered a lot. One day, in the hotel, she was walking along the corridor when another asylum seeker poured some hot tea on her. It caused a big ruckus and the police had to intervene. When the police came, they asked if I wanted the woman to be arrested and I said I did not. I declined her arrest because I knew that she was an unstable person. Moreover, she herself was an asylum seeker; and I was unaware of the kind of mental trauma that she might be undergoing. I did not know her situation, I did not know what she suffered in her country and why she had fled to the UK. Most asylum seekers had some sort of problem, and I did not want her to have any run-ins with the law. As a mother though, I was angry, and refused to see or speak to her. I had only one condition – I did not want her to continue staying in the same hotel as us. The authorities took her away and set her up in another place. My daughter who already had stress-induced urinary incontinence simply became worse because of that incident.

Throughout our stay in that London hotel, I did not sleep well. My husband tells me that I was anxious and depressed. I also realised that I was very stressed. How could I not be stressed when our safety was not guaranteed? Many distressing incidents occurred in that place. During the Christmas we spent there, the hotel was broken into by seven burglars who were on drugs. They went into rooms, terrified people and dispossessed them of their belongings. They did not come to our room because my husband refused to open the door.

The fears and stress, though they were real, were sometimes caused by insensitive and terrible actions. I remember a time when we opened our doors and saw a man covered in blood. He had cut himself because the Home Office denied his application for asylum. The blood flowed all over his face and chest. He was not the only one who did this. There were others who threw themselves down stairs so that an ambulance could be called for them, and they would not be removed from the UK. Then there were the fire alarms. Almost every night, somebody would set off a fire alarm either in jest or mistakenly. Imagine being asleep at two or three in the morning and being woken up and rushing outside the premises because a fire alarm had been triggered. Even if it was a false alarm, the protocol remained the same. Until the matter was investigated by the hotel to ensure it was a false alarm, we were not allowed to re-enter our rooms. I remember those days because my daughter would look at me with raw fear in her eyes and would ask, 'Mummy, mummy what happened?' Often, I myself did not know if the danger was real and could not answer. All we could do was follow protocol and instructions and it was the helplessness of our situation that was the most disturbing at such times.

Despite our refugee status, my children went to school, which was a daily one-hour commute on two buses. They had to travel from Vauxhall to Fulham Broadway, every day. Despite the distance, that school provided them with the only form of stability at the time. Changing schools to one closer would rob them of the one aspect of their lives in which they felt well-adjusted and stable. Also, we had left our life back in Algeria in search for peace. A good education is the tool by which my children – and children everywhere – could navigate a peaceful world. So, I used my own money – actually the money my sister gave me – and sent them on that commute every day. I resorted to getting money from my sister because the council was not ready to do more than they were already doing. But as many people know, the allowance we received weekly was not enough. The money we received in our hands each week was around £50 as a family and while the bus fare for the children was free, they had to be accompanied by an adult. This meant that we had to shell out £23 a week for bus fare for one of us to accompany our children.

Therefore, I had no option but to ask for financial assistance from my sister. The children's headteacher had informed us that our children were academically gifted and I had to ensure that I gave them the best chance possible to obtain a good education. My husband too was doing everything he could to keep us alive and well. If there were odd jobs to be done or errands to run, he was on hand. Yet, we could not afford some of the small pleasures of everyday life. If one of my children had a hankering for an ice cream, I could not get it because that ice cream money could buy us a bar of soap. These were the sort of decisions and choices we had to make at the time. Because of the privations of daily life, and the consumption of meals that largely lacked in nutrition, my children grew very lean in the course of those seventeen months. The relationship between my husband and I was also strained. To put it simply, we suffered.

Somewhere along the line, I asked the Home Office for better lodgings. The six of us could not continue to cram ourselves into a single room. In response, they provided us with two rooms, but they were not together. I was very uneasy about the rooms not being connected as it was very difficult for me to keep an eye on my children from a distance.

As an asylum seeker in the UK, your life is in the hands of the government. They could ask you to move at a moment's notice, and you have no choice. I have heard of people like us who have been moved three or four times. They had to move, leaving behind the connections they had formed in an attempt to create some semblance of rootedness or stability, only to find themselves in yet another new environment having to start from scratch. Thankfully, we have been moved only once, and it was from London to Swansea.

Around three months before I came to Swansea, I had a dream that the Home Office provided us with a house with the postcode SA16. That dream came true as we were indeed sent to live in a house with the very same postcode. In fact, the number of our house also turned out to be a number that was special to me because it was the date on which I was born. When the Home Office sent me the address and I saw the postcode, I told my husband that it was not a coincidence. I believed there was something for me in this new place and I wanted to come and find out what it was. I think the reason I dreamt about it is because I was suffering a lot and was constantly thinking about all the challenges and the changes that we had been through. I strongly believe that the universe heard me and helped me manifest this.

Since I have been living here, everything seems to be getting back on track. I can cook again and my love for cooking has returned. Cooking is how I express my joy of life and one could say that I am cooking to counteract all the inedible meals that we have had. Every other day, I am in the kitchen for hours, preparing food for my husband and children because I want to share my happiness in life with them. My family can feel my happiness and love in the food. In approximately a month after we got here, things changed and my children started to return to their normal weight and now look healthy. In fact, the school authorities reached out to me to say that they noticed the change in my children.

Now that I have some space and I can cook, I look back on my previous suffering, and have realised that I was like a fish out of water. In that hotel in London, my husband did not play any music. He was always running around, doing whatever jobs he could find to support us. The truth is that I was unable to support him because I was anxious and depressed. I was unable to do much in those days.

It took all my strength to simply survive and exist. My husband, was the one who was always having to be strong for our children and me. Now, the music is back. My husband plays the guitar, and is in a band, which plays their music at events and bars around Swansea. My skills as a chef are back and we are expressing happiness the best way we know how.

Like any other place, Swansea has a mix of all sorts of people, good and bad. But I choose to see only the good in people and feel only the good energy in this place. Sometimes, I take long walks by the sea, and enjoy the gift of nature and smell the sea. The thing about Swansea is that though some people may seem averse to strangers, they also listen to people's stories and give them a chance, which is a blessing.

I am like a flower that has now found its life source in water. And I am blooming and glowing.

My English is not very good yet, but it is gradually getting better. As I interact more with people and make more of an effort, it will get better.

Though we have not been granted refugee status, we have hope. My husband and I are young, and are willing to work – to do whatever it takes to give our children a good life. We are not looking for handouts, we do not seek free housing or food, just freedom to live, to love, and to shine.

# Comparisons, Contexts and Conflict

## Arafa Dafalla

From the very beginning of my life, I seemed to have been destined for a life in an international environment despite my Sudanese heritage. Born in Greece in 1997, we moved to Sudan for two years, after which we spent five years in The Netherlands until the age of eight. I unfortunately do not have many memories of my life in The Netherlands. Following this, we moved back to Sudan for a further four years, eventually emigrating to Wales at the age of twelve – I have been living in Wales for the past twelve years now.

I am visually impaired and had cataract surgery when I was just six months old. I also suffer from Glaucoma nystagmus. Coping with my impairment has been an integral part of my early and young adult years and I often end up weighing up the positives and negatives of living in Sudan and my life in Wales within the context of my disability.

Before coming to the UK, I had heard from friends and acquaintances that it was an 'extraordinary' country and one that people dream of living in. As a result, my expectations were quite high, and I was very excited to move to Wales. However, my excitement was a bit dampened as we drove to Cardiff in the summer of my twelfth year, for the weather, the roads, the architecture of the buildings all seemed familiar. It brought back the few memories I had of living in The Netherlands and I wondered whether life in Wales would also be similar to The Netherlands. While at first glance, the UK seemed familiar to me, in my young mind I had expected more on account of the various, highly enthusiastic accounts of the country I had heard from others.

As we settled into life in Cardiff, I became nostalgic for my life in Sudan. I no longer had the freedoms that I had enjoyed in Sudan, especially in terms of going outdoors alone. My parents had to accompany me everywhere I went, even if it was just to the park. In our Sudanese village of Al Dabiba, an hour out of the capital Khartoum, where I spent a few years of my childhood, it was very safe and, as is usually the case in most village settings, everyone knew each other. It took both my sister and me some time to get used to the change. In fact, in our early days in Cardiff, my sister caused some concern in school and at home. She walked home alone after school as she had been used to doing in Sudan. This caused some panic at school and at home and my parents had to impress on us the potential dangers of simply heading outdoors alone in our new environment. In Sudan, I had a thriving group of friends with whom I spent most of my free time. Since moving to Wales, I lost touch with them on account of there not being any social media in Sudan when we moved to Wales. We depended entirely on Skype to maintain our connection with family and friends, which was not always the most convenient medium.

The upshot however, is that we now live in the pretty region of Llanishen with leafy roads and parks. Llanishen is a northern district of Cardiff and therefore, close to all the major amenities that a big city has to offer. We are also fortunate to reside in a large house with a garden that we all make use of the most in the summer and whenever the weather permits. This at least, mitigated some of the restrictiveness and lack of safety that my siblings and I felt, when compared to the freedom of going out and about with ease on our own during our time in Sudan.

While my siblings began their studies in Wales in the new school year in the local school, I did not start school until January of the following year as I was registered in a school that had all the necessary facilities and equipment to aid me with my education, given my visual impairment. I recall visiting the school for the first time with my father and I also remember being very nervous and anxious, as I did not know what to expect. I was handed a sheet of paper on which there were many scattered dots and asked to feel them. This was my introduction to Braille. My first few months in my new school were rather unnerving, as I did not know anyone and had not made any friends. I did not join the rest of my classmates in the classroom since I needed to first learn English with the teaching assistant in a separate room using Braille. It was only when I had gained some mastery over the English language that I was permitted to join the rest of my class. All of this was a very novel experience for me. In Sudan our primary school was small, and only held eight classrooms, one for each year. All subjects were taught in the same classroom, whereas here, my school was far larger and the system of learning was quite different.

I was hesitant and quiet initially – I felt like my classmates would poke fun at my English since I was not totally fluent. In Sudan, I had felt far more comfortable in class and I was much more talkative and even a little mischievous. Having said this, my early days in my new high school in Wales did also remind me somewhat of my early days of school in Sudan. We had moved from The Netherlands to Sudan and I had to learn to read and write Arabic since the lessons were through the medium of Arabic. Nevertheless, I had found it easier to settle into my new class environment in Sudan than I did in Llanedeyrn High School. I found myself comparing my two schools in many ways. In Sudan, the respect for teachers in the classroom was paramount, and pupils would never dare to answer back or be rude, whereas this was not always the case in my school in Cardiff. In fact, I remember an instance where a pupil dared to throw a pair of scissors at one of our teachers, something that shocked me greatly.

Even the way the class was structured was different in Sudan, for boys and girls sat separately on each side of the class and did not mix. However, one of the things I absolutely despised during my school days in Sudan was that punishment for even minor offences such as arriving late, failing a test, not doing our homework, to name a few, was very harsh and disproportionate and pupils were hit with a stick to keep them in line. I used to walk to school with my friend and we often arrived late, but in order to avoid corporal punishment, we used to jump over the wall and sneak in. Due to the threat of punishment, we took our studies very seriously and spent a lot of time on our schoolwork. We were also given several poems or verses from the Quran to memorise on a regular basis. In contrast, in my new school in Cardiff, the schoolwork in general was easier and we were not given much homework. Exams too began only during Year Ten. I felt that the standard of education when compared with all that we were taught at a much younger age was far harder in Sudan. For instance, I was truly surprised to find that in some cases even pupils sixteen years of age were not well-versed with their times tables, whereas in Sudan, we had to memorise these when we were aged seven. Such differences in the style and content of education as well as the difference in the school culture and environment added to my anxiety and period of time it took me to adjust to my new school in Cardiff.

The facilities and equipment at Llanedeyrn High School, truly eased the process of obtaining my education. My old school in Sudan lacked the facilities for disabilities such as mine, and I relied heavily on the help I received from my friends in class as well as my aunt and my mother. Unfortunately, the awareness of disabilities and visual impairments was not high amongst my classmates in my school in Sudan and I was the target of much bullying. Sometimes, the other children snatched my glasses from my face and laughed at the involuntary movements of my eyes which is a characteristic of my particular eye condition. Those were very upsetting times and I often wondered why God had made me so different to everyone else around me, and why I had to suffer this disability.

In Llanedeyrn High School, I had been in and amongst predominantly white classmates, but when I was in the sixth form,

I moved to Fitzalan School, where there were quite a few Muslim pupils. In fact, I met my best friend there who is also visually impaired. For the first time in my life, I was able to share my feelings and emotions with someone who understood exactly how I felt, with whom I felt comfortable sharing, something I had never been able to do even with my own parents. When we shared our experiences, it lessened the sometimes overwhelming sentiments of feeling different and inadequate.

The teaching assistants at Fitzalan introduced us to The Royal National Institute of Blind People (RNIB), which had a wide range of equipment to aid us with our studies and everyday lives. It was also heartening and a large confidence boost to see that many of the volunteers and staff working with RNIB are also visually impaired and it raised my optimism levels. To think that despite my impairment, there are opportunities for meaningful employment in the workplace was a source of much hope for the future. I soon joined a phone group run by RNIB called 'Women with Vision', which consists of relatively young Muslim women with visual impairments from various countries. Despite our different geographical origins, we all found common cultural aspects, which bound us together apart from our obvious shared experience of being visually impaired. The group used to meet once a month especially during COVID and this provided us all with the much-needed social interactions that we had all been craving.

I do find it difficult to entirely understand some of the norms of life in the UK in general however, which are quite the opposite of the culture in Sudan. For one, I feel the all-encompassing respect for parents that Islam teaches us, seems to be watered down in Wales. Children usually leave their parents' homes at the age of eighteen and in due course, set up their own homes and lead more or less entirely independent lives. Later on in life, when their parents need assistance as they age, children often place them in a residential or care home instead of looking after their parents themselves as is the case in Sudan. I also find that it tends to be a more individualistic society here in Wales because there is not as much familial contact as there is in Sudan. Here, families come together mainly for pivotal occasions such as Christmas or Easter, whereas in Sudan, my entire family would gather at my grandmother's home every Friday, be it my immediate family or my extended family. Proximity for sure made this possible, but even for those who live further away, the central focus is still the larger family structure. There are always exceptions and I realise that I am generalising, but my observations are entirely based on my personal experience and encounters.

On the other hand, I am so grateful to be living in Wales as a disabled person, because here, people understand disabilities and mental health issues and do their utmost to help and make life as easy as possible for those who are afflicted with any sort of impairment or disability. It makes me very sad to consider just how different the situation is in Sudan in relation to disabilities and mental health issues. Family members who are disabled or impaired are sometimes even hidden away because the families are ashamed of them. People with any disability of impairment are sometimes considered as burdens to the family and non-contributing members of society, as there are little or no opportunities for them to flourish or become physically and financially independent. I often wonder how different my life would have been if my family and I had still lived in Sudan. I certainly would not have been able to complete my schooling or have the same opportunity to contemplate getting married in the future and living a normal life. I would have been dependent on my parents for even the smallest of things.

In Wales, I was able to enrol for a Psychology degree at university. Even though I only managed to complete my first year and had to drop out due to excessive stress, I was still given the opportunity to finish my degree if I had wished. It was a different matter that I found it difficult to fit into university life as a Muslim woman who did not drink alcohol or go to parties. In the first year at university, I found that this was mostly what my peers were interested in.

Learning was not the priority, for very few attended lectures regularly. It was an environment that required much adjustment on my part and while I was there, resulted in a lot of anxiety and stress since I felt like a misfit.

On the whole however, I enjoy my life in Cardiff. It is a multicultural society, providing me with opportunities I would never have had if I had remained in Sudan. I have got to meet people from various parts of the world, and enjoyed learning about their cultures, their language and food. All in all, my horizons have been broadened tremendously since I moved to Wales, something that would have been difficult to achieve if we had never left Sudan.

Furthermore, given the current political climate in Sudan and the ongoing civil war, I feel truly blessed to be living safely in Wales, despite our constant worry for our family in Al Dabiba. Being situated so close to the capital Khartoum, places it in a potentially volatile region, but fortunately it has not had to suffer any military intervention or destruction to date. My family and the other residents of the village however, have been living with power cuts (and as a result, poor phone communications), as well as food and water shortages. At the start of the conflict, my family in Cardiff was glued to the events unfolding back in Sudan on the Al Jazeera news network and watched the people being evacuated. In fact, two of the people evacuated happened to be my cousin and her one-year-old child. Universities and schools, including my old school in Al Dabiba have been disrupted due to the conflict. Some Khartoum University students who could afford to switch over to other universities in Africa, such as Egypt, Tanzania, etc. have done so, but those who are unable to afford the expense are now able to continue or complete their higher education in universities in other parts of Sudan that are less affected by the civil war. A friend who is now in her last year of her medical degree has had it particularly hard. She began her degree in 2019 during the revolution and the continuous protests disrupted her classes. Soon after, COVID struck and all classes shifted to the online platform – and now it is the civil war. She is hoping to go to a small island university near Tanzania to finally finish her medical degree. I see very little, if any, efforts by the international community, be it the UN or other major Muslim countries to moderate via diplomacy or assist in providing a resolution, which is exceedingly disheartening. Given that the majority of my extended family including my grandmother live there, the underlying anxiety for their safety is persistent. Many either did not want to leave at the start of the conflict or then were physically unable to leave, as is the case with my grandmother – and now of course, it is extremely difficult practically to leave in the midst of the conflict. In Al Dabiba now, the situation is comparatively stable and some of my parents' friends from Khartoum have managed to move temporarily to the village until the conflict ends. At a time like this, the spirit of humanity and overwhelming desire to help each other is paramount.

No one should ever underestimate the incredible blessing of being safe and feeling safe. During my childhood years, I took for granted the safety and freedom of living in a village in Sudan. And now, more than ever, I am appreciative of all that living in Wales, a relatively quiet and safe part of the world, has bestowed upon me.

# 'Covering' My Life

## Sweeta Durani

When I came to the UK in 2018, I had not planned to never return home. It was a picture of me in the news that changed the course of my journey, left me out here alone and without the protective embrace of my loved ones.

I got married at thirteen; it was a forced marriage. Although I was coerced into the union, it was standard fare for Afghan girls to be sent into matrimony at a very young age. In some cases, girls were married off at the onset of their menses; while some others were sent away for more capricious whims. Every teen bride was essentially a child whose whole childhood was yanked away from her, and her life changed even though she often did not even understand the implications of it.

Even though I was still a child, I was soon responsible for another human. I had my first child at fourteen, barely a year into my marriage. I had another child four years later. As a child who was now a parent, I quickly realised that I had to manage and be responsible for everything in my life. I had no one to teach me or manage anything my behalf. Sometimes, I would get a little sympathy; but sympathy is not kindness, and is never permanent. So, I learnt to fight for my life.

In the main, Afghan women do not work. They stay at home all day cooking, cleaning, caring for children, and tending to the needs of the men in their households. They neither have a voice nor space for expression. It was the same for me. In my family, my father-in-law forbade me from going out. If I needed to leave home, I would be chaperoned, clad in a *burqa* and forbidden from interacting with men outside my family. The chaperone would be a man – usually my husband or somebody appointed by him. I felt stifled and wanted to do something – I wanted to work.

There were exceptions to this ethos, in the same way as light finds the means to pierce the thickest darkness. There are families in Afghanistan who are more liberal, who know the worth of work, and the value of every soul – male and female – that aspire to make something better of themselves. Such families, though few, encourage their daughters to be what they want, and become what they envisage for themselves. It is like being the only one in a marathon running in the right direction, and without applause. My father and the family he built is one such case. My impetus to work came from home.

Finding a job meant that I had to fight my husband's family. Though women were not allowed to work outside the home, I persisted. I remember being asked why I wanted to persist in this endeavour; I told them that it was something I had to do. Perhaps, they eventually allowed me to work because I would be working with women in a setting where men were not allowed.

To get to work, I had to walk a long distance from my home to the office and back every day, because I was not allowed to board a bus or take a taxi, so that I would not have any contact with men. I would be fully covered as I walked this long distance. At work, I could divest myself of the robes because we were all women there, and men were not allowed in the office, as our work revolved around women. We worked to promote women's rights and taught them skills like making jewellery so that they could earn some money and embark on their journey towards self-sufficiency.

It was impossible not to meet with men though, because all the laws in Afghanistan – even those specifically targeted towards women – are made by men. Therefore, as I advocated women's rights, the people to speak with, who had the power to affect any real change in women's lives and their affairs, were men.

When my husband and his family saw that I was making some money for myself and my children, things became potentially fatal for me. They would trouble me and try to stop me from going to work, and they would threaten and manhandle my children to deter me, but I would not stop. Instead, all these privations spurred me on towards the path of activism. Having financial independence and the freedom that came with it, made my spirit soar. If I baulked in the face of trouble, I would avoid some discomfort. But if I faced my challenges head-on, I would still have to face opposition, but good things could come out of the situation. Even if I did not directly benefit from the situation, I would still be left with life lessons and experience. So, I persevered and began to explore other parts of myself.

I love to write, so I wrote. I wrote reports, news, and conducted research for local media. It was yet another earning stream, as I got paid for my writing and research, which I enjoyed. Once, I was even invited by the local media platform, but this made my life at home difficult once my family saw me in a public space. I started writing on social media in Afghanistan, and my writing brought me some visibility. I gradually became a household name among Afghan women and some men. My husband and his family did not like the visibility I was achieving, so they harassed me and my children even more. However, the more they harassed us, the more I persevered; the better things got for me and my children.

There are people in Afghanistan, women and even some men, who are open-minded. My father was such a man. It did not matter to my father that I was a girl, especially in a place where people were sometimes disappointed when girls were born. My father sent me to school and asked me to work like an ordinary citizen despite the restrictions and taboos that accompanied women's movement and visibility. He encouraged me to reach for whatever I wanted, and promised to support me in any way he could. He encouraged me to stand with my head high. May my father's memory be blessed. He passed away at a time when I needed him the most. However, though he was no longer with us, his teachings imbued me and gave me the impetus to forge on.

In my activism and social work, I told women and whoever would listen, that the only jobs available for women in Afghanistan were cooking, cleaning, bearing children, and keeping house. Men in general, knew nothing about the significance of women's roles in the family. Perhaps, if men and women had the same opportunities to work and if men were at home more to see what keeping the home entailed, they would understand the opposite sex more, and display some compassion.

In addition to my activism, writing and social work, I decided to start a business. In starting the business, I asked for my friend's help. She would be a front for the business; the business would bear her name, and I would appear to work for her. She agreed, and my husband and his family did not have any issues with this, since I would not be working for a man. Thankfully, the jewellery business thrived and flourished encompassing the joy and sense of freedom that its logo of the dancing woman, designed by me, represented.

Apart from freedom, our business logo of a dancing woman also represents women not being ashamed to be themselves. The ability of women to express their hopes, dreams, aspirations, and challenges is captured in it. When I am stressed or hard-pressed, I often dance. Dancing, for me, is a way of escape. Therefore, the act of dancing in the logo is meant to represent the woman and the freedom she should have, as well as her peculiar methods for soaring high in life. After the success of this business, I embarked on another one, which also thrived. I moved from walking long distances to work, to owning a car and driving myself around the city.

My team and I held many programmes and seminars to promote women's economic and social development. I faced all the challenges that existed in Afghanistan head-on, especially the ones that women dealt with, and I had achieved relative success in work and education. For this reason, the British Embassy in Kabul made a documentary of my activities, which was screened at the Embassy in Kabul itself and is also available on YouTube.

Later, because of my two active and successful businesses in Herat, I was invited to a business conference called 'She Trades', which was for women only and was sponsored by UNDP (United Nations Development Programme). Businesses and business owners from fifty-seven countries came to Liverpool, and I was one of them. Being invited to such a conference was not new to me. I had already been on many such business and educational trips in different countries such as the USA, China, Tajikistan, and India.

Participating in this conference resulted in a new page opening in my life. A photo of me without a *hijab* and the news from the conference was spread on web pages and Afghan news, because the First Lady of Afghanistan also participated in that conference. This caused a lot of problems for me because my husband and his family did not know that I had gone to this conference. I was not supposed to travel out of the country without a male family member. Things got so heated that I took the difficult decision to stay back in the UK. Returning to Afghanistan was tantamount to losing my life. So, I put aside all the hard work and everything I had fought for for years, and only thought about saving my life, and the lives of my two children, my mother and my sisters. I then applied for asylum.

Five years have passed, and when I remember those days, I still feel physical pain. The understanding that people give up all their possessions and attachments to save their lives can only be understood by people who have gone through these experiences. It does not matter if people migrate by choice or out of compulsion; it still hurts. At least, the people who leave their homes behind to make a new life elsewhere, are somewhat prepared. I did not even bring personal belongings that would last me for more than a few days. This kind of forced displacement takes everything out of a person, leaving behind nothing but a hollow place that was once filled with love, personality, interests, friends and family. Sometimes, the space left is full of things whose echoes only reverberate in dour tones: echoes of worry, fear, loss, and sometimes, a little glimpse of a silver lining.

After the difficult events of those days, I got the good news that I had been granted a few months to remain in the UK as a refugee. I was happy and started working to bring my family over. Once the photo of me circulated at home, I told my mother 'Please, just save my children.' I begged my friend to give them a home. I had made plans with another friend to move my children, mother, and sisters to Pakistan for their safety. I did this because things could get fatal if my husband and my father-in-law got to them first.

I pulled myself together, and enthusiastically started studying, learning English and building a new life in this country. I successfully completed the first and second years of college and was selected as the student of the year. Besides my studies and work, I volunteered every day and continued to find ways for my family to join me. Five years had passed, and all of them were not here yet.

Little by little, my mental condition worsened, and the loneliness and worry for my children and family living in a tenuous position where their security and safety were concerned, made my mental condition deteriorate to such an extent that I was unable to complete my last year of university. There were many reasons why my family, even my children, could not come. COVID-19 pandemic conditions caused everything to be shut down, and work stopped. The inefficiency of the lawyer meant that their application was rejected. After that, I tried again, but the war in Ukraine started, and no one cared about my story and the difficult conditions my children and family were going through. It felt like no one heard my voice, and I could not do anything. I always thought that one day I would help Afghan women and my people to solve many problems. Instead, I become a person who had no support or agency.

The time of the pandemic especially, was a difficult period for me. All doors were closed, and all connections were cut off. During the lockdown, I was depressed, anxious, and isolated. I was only able to stay alive because of the thought of my children and loved ones.

However, after a dark night comes the dawn. One day, while thinking about all those who could possibly help me, I remembered friends like Jeni and Jill, and contacted them. I had several counselling sessions with Jill. I also made some new friends who supported me and my family. The support has grown from strength to strength, and a petition has been started for my family. After four years of trying, my children got their visas and were reunited with me. My mother and sisters, however, are still in disarray, and I still worry a lot about them.

2023 has been a positive year for me – as they say, I am beginning to rise now after the fall. Good days are gradually returning. These days I am busy with many online classes and am trying to make the most of all the opportunities here. The Welsh government is training us in business. I hope I can start my business again after this training. Other positive things have also occurred this year. I have written some articles and some poems, and I have even dabbled in art. One of my art works, 'Let Us Go and We Hugged Each Other More Tightly', is a celebration of all the strong women who have helped me along this journey. First, my mother, who gave birth to me and who still remains in the shackles of oppression, waiting to be free. Then, the good women with whom I trekked long distances to work and with whom I have championed the cause for women. My friend, whose name serves as the front for my business in Afghanistan, and another friend, who at short notice, took my family in, gave them refuge, and continues to provide a home for them these past years. Then, there are Jill and Jen, and the countless women who have transcended the boundary of friendship and have become sisters to me in this country, bringing their love and light to lighten my burden.

There is a picture in my heart. It is a good picture. I picture a day when my mother and sisters will come out here and experience life in all its glory and freedom. I keep looking at my phone screen, waiting for the news of their imminent arrival. Then my life will seem complete.

Till that day comes, I will continue my work. Though I cannot go to Afghanistan, I can reach Afghanistan through social media. Consequently, I have decided that I will write whatever I can, produce whatever art I can, dance whenever I can, sing whenever I can, teach whenever I can and speak out as loud as I can so that more women and children can be free. I also dream that perhaps one day, we will have more men who will see the light, come over to our side, and be agents of freedom. That would be the day.

# No Time to Change the World: The Journey of a Social Worker from Dhaka to Cardiff

**Tahmina Khan**

When I came to Wales for the first time in 1980, I was only twenty years old and did not speak a word of English. I was studying geography at Dhaka University at the time, a field I had enrolled in just because I got admission into the University and wanted to join it, irrespective of the subject I had to study. I used to excel in Chemistry and would have switched my major subject in my second year, but then I got married to a man who lived in Wales and ended up moving countries to be with him.

My father passed away when I was sixteen, and I was raised by my older brothers. They wanted me to move to the United Kingdom to live a 'better life', and they also ended up moving to the West after marriage. I had five brothers, but two of them were martyred in the 1971 war between East Pakistan and West Pakistan; a war that resulted in the creation of Bangladesh. My brothers live around the world now, and I live in Wales. We have three children, who were all raised in Wales and now live with their own families in London.

Today, I am a social worker in Cardiff and have been for the last thirty years after successfully earning a degree in that subject and have created a name for myself in the world of fostering services amongst ethnically diverse communities in Wales. Here is my story.

**My struggle with English**

From the young age of two or three, we were taught to write in English but there was no focus on spoken English. I struggled to translate words from my language (Bengali) to English, which I cannot even imagine now. But at the time I really struggled with the spoken language and I was just thrown into the deep end when I moved to Wales with my husband.

My husband had been a student at the University of Cardiff at first and then he worked as an electrical engineer. He changed jobs after that, but the company closed down so he lost his job and decided to start his own venture. As soon as I came with him to Wales, we started a corner grocery shop in the January of 1982. Sometimes when he went out shopping or ran other chores like going to the bank in the daytime, I would look after the shop. People would come in and ask me complex questions, and I would never understand them. I could not understand or speak the language beyond the basics. In fact, I look at my nieces and nephews in Bangladesh today and the education system has advanced so much, they are all fluent in English now. At the time when I was growing up in Bangladesh, the education system did not treat English as a priority, and everything functioned through the medium of Bengali. Schools and universities were not private at the time and were all owned by the State focusing more on the Bengali language. The media also used Bengali, and I did not have the support or the opportunity then to become fluent in English.

Having said that, I learnt that when you are put on the spot, you learn quickly. In Cardiff, I decided to join classes to learn English as a Second Language. In fact, I wanted to continue my studies and take O level and A level examinations, but there was a financial issue. I would have had to pay a fee to take these examinations, since it was privately administered. As a result, I decided to let go of this idea until I pursued a diploma in Social Work in 1993.

**Working for the community**

After completing a diploma in Social Work, I started engaging in social work and activities related to it in order to qualify as a social worker. Our neighbourhood was full of Asian people, and I had already started doing voluntary work with them. For instance, many women at the time could not read letters from their General Practitioner (GP) or solicitors, especially if there was some dispute related to their marriage. These women used to come to me to seek help in order to respond to these letters or make an appointment with their GP. I started getting very involved with them, even though I was raising my own young children at the time. I enjoyed helping out women who did not know English, sometimes even voluntarily going in with them for a doctor's appointment to help with interpretation. During this time, I picked up a lot of spoken English through sheer practice. Even as far back as 1990, I was engaged in short employment stints and involved with the community. In fact, we started running an association to support Asian women, where we met weekly and discussed issues faced by them.

In 1990, there was a job advertised by a leading British charity. They were building a multicultural resource centre for ethnically diverse women. I became deeply involved in helping to build this women's centre and started thinking about culturally sensitive issues and decisions such as creating separate prayer or meditation rooms. The whole steering group used to work closely with the architect and builders. When the building opened in 1991, I was employed with them as a part-time project worker after an interview process. The charity also had a training and recruitment scheme for ethnically diverse women and, in 1993, I was seconded by this organisation to pursue a training course. I was privileged to be one of ten employees selected to attend this programme.

I ended up working at this charity for twenty-five years on the same project, but in different settings. I even went to London for two years to the Head Office as an IT trainer. I worked in multiple fields, but in my last role which I held for sixteen years, I was working in family placement, fostering and adoption. I left the charity in 2016, and from 2016 to 2018, I worked with a private fostering agency, and then from 2019 onwards, I began working with a fostering organisation as a senior practitioner. In this role, I felt I found my calling and I am still working in the same space. As a part of my role, I recruit and assess foster carers, recruit them, approve them, and support them when children are placed with them.

**Assimilating and integrating**
My life and work in the UK has of course brought me into professional and personal contact with local Welsh and white people and I have formed close friendships with many of them over the years. In fact, in my early days in Cardiff, while on the one hand my husband and I faced overt, in-our-face racist slogans thrown at us, simultaneously, I was helped a lot by a local woman and her granddaughter, in improving my English-speaking skills, for which I am very grateful. However, I have also felt, especially in my professional capacity, that there was the tendency to place the entire responsibility of any ethnic minority fostering family or foster child on ethnically diverse employees such as myself, rather than trying to also understand the intricacies of cultural norms for themselves. It seemed almost like the easier option to hand over such cases to people like me.

I feel that while it is possible to integrate into the local society in which we are living, it is difficult to fully assimilate as the nuances of varied ethnically diverse customs and traditions are very rarely communicated, or rather, it is often difficult to fully communicate these nuances to a community that is culturally, historically, and linguistically so different from our own. In other words, we are often unable to impart our norms and culture entirely, and the local community often fails to obtain a deeper understanding of us. I feel that a different value system tends to always stand out as a different value system, regardless of the number of decades that we spent living within a certain system of norms and culture. Therefore, it is difficult to fully assimilate if we still hold dear our original value system, which is part of our origin, inherent culture and part of who we are as a person. Integrating into my local community has not been a problem at all, but at the end of the day, because of the sentiments expressed above, my loyalty will always lie with my ethnic minority brethren. Having said that, I do feel that this is natural, and it is often the case even if our roles are reversed, i.e. if white people settle in another country, they often socialise with other white people.

Life for ethnic minority or ethnically diverse people in Wales is not all hunky-dory. Career progression for ethnic minority people is still difficult. In my own experience, I have found that being promoted to managerial ranks is still less likely for black and ethnic minority people than white people, even though the latter might lack the experience. I have been qualified as a social worker since 1995, and have gained immense experience over the years. But at the same time, I have not felt rewarded for my work and in fact, I feel like I am treated differently from newly qualified workers. Additionally, I also feel a bit excluded on account of not participating in the social life of the office. As a Muslim, the culture of drinking is one I do not enter into, and I often feel left out of the easy rapport that many of my white colleagues share due to their social interactions. Things might be a bit different in England, but I have always felt that there is much racism and discrimination still evident in Wales. We, as Asians, often lack confidence and tend to be more submissive, which is perhaps a legacy of colonialism.

I am now over sixty years old, and still have a few more years of working in the community. I have considered challenging the system at times, but I know that if I go down that route, I will probably end up in tribunal courts or being involved in an expensive legal battle. I have not got the time to change the world, and I am happy continuing to do the work that I enjoy doing, even though sometimes we need to work twice as hard to succeed.

## The darker reality of social work

I have been working closely with another organisation as a chair currently. I have worked with them as a founder member since their inception. This has grown from three to four staff members when it started, to over hundred staff members now with offices in Cardiff, Swansea, Newport, and other places. I have always been supportive of this organisation to seek and receive more funding. Our main core funding comes from the Welsh government. This organisation is very well known and recognised now as one of the leading organisations in its sector in Wales. My greatest takeaway from my job in this sector is the difference I am able to make to the lives of women in the community, but I have encountered many unsafe situations in this field of work as well. We have dealt with many situations where women are alone, divorced or being really ill-treated by their husbands or families; and then not having the confidence to seek a divorce or not being able to walk away because their passport has been hidden or their immigration has not been sorted out. They are constantly under threat from their in-laws and their husbands.

I work quite closely with the Bangladeshi community of women as well and have faced a lot of ire from the men in the community. I have been labelled as the 'trouble-maker' in the community as there is the perception that I encourage women to rebel against the system. There was a phone call to my employer complaining that I create problems in the community, and even included fabricated allegations against me relating to my personal life. The men became so fearful that they were losing control that they resorted to extreme measures and as a result, I have been bad-mouthed in the community, because they know I am working to empower the vulnerable women in their families. They say things such as 'Oh, Tahmina, don't talk about her, she is too dangerous for our women. She gets women out of the house and breaks up their marriages.' But when the women come to us, their marriages are already in danger.

Sometimes, it is only a matter of supporting women to become more confident through skills and training in self-development. Some of the women in the community are provided with transport to come for our regular meetings or learn how to drive and gain other life skills and become financially independent. In fact, women have shared their stories of choosing their own partners after coming out of a very abusive relationship or marriage, and that feels extremely encouraging. We are working towards putting policies in place to safeguard women in these situations and provide them with a safety net when they have no support after walking out of a difficult or abusive marriage.

**Looking ahead**
My concern in my career has always been about making a difference to the families in my community, more than tracking my own career progression. I should have been a manager by this stage of my career, but I deliberately never applied for that role because I have always wanted to be involved at the grassroots level, working closely with the families and cases, as this gives me immense satisfaction. In fact, if I was promoted to a managerial role, I would not be able to remain as involved with the community, working with the families and with the children one-to-one. I may not be at the highest level professionally, but personally I feel I have achieved a lot in my job and I am confident in my abilities. I am respected as a chair of the organisation I work with, and people take me seriously, and that is more than enough for me.

In the future, I envision setting up a counselling service for black and Asian children in Wales. There is no such service in Cardiff at all and there are so many young black and Asian people who are grappling with issues such as identity crises; who have got no communication with their own families; who have developed mental health issues as a result of not being able to fit in; to name but a few. My colleagues and I are working on this, and we want to develop this counselling service in the future. This has been a challenge to work on along with a full-time job, since it is a huge responsibility and one has to be registered as a company and audited by Welsh families. It needs a lot of safeguarding as well, and it will be difficult to run a financially viable agency, but we can start with ten sets of foster families and move forward from there. Setting up a counselling service for young people from ethnically diverse communities, run by people from ethnically diverse communities, is important as others will not understand or empathise with their issues in the same way.

Cardiff is smaller than London and it will be easier to set up a new organisation here rather than in a big city. But at the same time, it would be easier to get resources and support in a big city like London or Birmingham. When I look into different projects in these cities, they are so much more advanced than those in Cardiff. I feel sometimes that we are lagging way behind and have not made much difference in terms of setting up organisations here. We have a lot to learn from them, their community centres and the services they are providing. I hope to fulfil my dream of starting my own counselling service, to continue my work towards the community and leave a lasting impression in the field of social work, aimed particularly at ethnically diverse communities in the UK.

# 'Miss my country but this feels like home': A Story from Syria

## Latifa Najjar

In February 2023, there was a devastating earthquake in Syria. This was a 7.8 magnitude earthquake, one of the largest in the Turkey-Syria region. This took over 8,000 lives and injured over 14,500 people in Syria. It is estimated that over five million people were made homeless after this disaster. To read this news from a distance was shocking and heart-breaking for all of us who have been forced to live outside our country.

When this happened, I wanted to do something for my people back home. So I hosted an event in Wales. This was a dinner event organised to raise funds to support victims of the earthquake in my home country. We were able to raise over £3,000 through that event, and since then, I have felt so proud that I have been able to do something for my country albeit from afar. I try to do something for people in need through whatever means I have today, and I am always happy when I can do something for people, especially in my hometown. It was not easy to move so far away from home...

### Arriving in Aberystwyth

'The Syrian refugees who fled war now cooking their way into the hearts of a Welsh community,' reads a headline of an article in Wales Online from 28 May 2020 about my life. It goes on to say, 'Worlds away from the war-ravaged streets and scorching heat of Damascus, the capital of Syria, is the historic seaside town of Aberystwyth in mid-Wales. But these two worlds have come together after a number of refugee families from Syria moved to Ceredigion in recent years.'

It was November 2016 when I arrived in Aberystwyth for the first time. I had grown up in the city of Homs, in central Western Syria, where I studied design. I got married after finishing my studies, but unfortunately, only a year after my marriage, we had to flee the country because of the growing political unrest. We were so happy before the war but then my hometown was destroyed, and we had to leave the country. We left Syria in 2013 and moved to Egypt initially, along with many others who also had to escape the violence and unrest at home. In fact, my first child was born there twelve years ago now, but she was only two years old when we left Egypt, so she does not remember much.

We ended up living in Cairo for three and a half years, until UNICEF brought us to Wales. We were brought to Ceredigion in particular, thanks to the support of the British Red Cross under the Syrian Resettlement Scheme. The aim of this project was to bring 20,000 refugees into the country between 2015 and 2020. In fact, Ceredigion County Council surpassed its target of resettling fifty Syrian refugees fleeing the Syrian conflict, by homing fifty-four individuals in the area by November 2019 (Wales Online 2020). These statistics are heart-warming for us to see, and makes us feel even more at home in this county, since everyone has always stood by us and supported us here. In fact, in all of Wales, over a thousand Syrian families have made a home here thanks to local authorities signing up to welcome them. We are grateful for this every day.

Aberystwyth feels familiar to me. While some people might complain about the weather and find it difficult to adapt, the weather here actually makes me feel closer to my hometown. Believe it or not, the weather and temperatures here are practically the same in winter as in Syria. Summer temperatures in the two regions however, cannot be compared. For me, the weather has not been a challenge at all. If at all there is a challenge, it is to do with language and I am trying my best to navigate that by getting better at it every day.

**Speaking the language**

We were given a two-bedroom house in Aberystwyth, which had one living room and a kitchen. My parents received another house to live in and they live very close to me in town. Our landlord was extremely kind and helpful and was an excellent host as we arrived in this new place for the first time. I did not speak English and it was very difficult for me to adjust in the country. Initially, there were women who were brought in to translate and interpret for us from Arabic, as we were struggling with speaking the language when we first arrived. There was a lady who stayed with us for three days but once she left, we had to start going to college to learn English. I had learnt English in Syria as well, one lesson a week, but what I learnt was not sufficient to negotiate life here. We were not taught in a formal manner, and I had not learnt to speak it fluently. It did not help me read or write or even understand people when they spoke in English. I needed a lot more support when I got here.

After six months of learning English, I felt a little more confident. I went to Coleg Ceredigion, where the teachers were wonderful and supportive towards my learning journey. The Welsh people have always been so kind. They offered to help us improve our English, so that we could understand people around us better and speak some English with them. As a result of this, I started making a lot of friends in the town, and started becoming a part of the community. I found that people in Aberystwyth were extremely friendly, and they were available for help whenever I needed them. It slowly started to feel like we were amongst family, whom we could reach out to in times of sickness or any other problem. The welcoming people and community, along with the fantastic scenery around and nature as well as the fact that it is an extremely safe environment here for us and our children, are some of the most endearing aspects of living here in Aberystwyth.

Apart from English, there was also the need to learn Welsh in Aberystwyth since it is a strongly Welsh-speaking town. I learnt a few words only, such as *Bore Da* and *Croeso*, but not much more. I have three children now, and they go to Plascrug School in Aberystwyth. They have learnt to speak Welsh in school, along with English and they speak Arabic at home. I send them to Arabic school every week too, because I believe it is important for them to grow up with a sense of their own language and identity. I know that Welsh people also believe strongly in a sense of identity attached to the language, and that is inspiring for me. Interestingly, there are some sounds in the Welsh alphabet that are similar to Arabic, like the 'ch' sound, so it makes it easier for us all to get to grips with the phonetics of it. It is exciting to make these discoveries in a culture that we always imagined was so different from our own. My children are growing up multilingual. I arrived here with two daughters who are now twelve and ten, and my son (three) was born in Wales. This is why I am always busy and active; there is a lot to manage between the three of them. After all, I am only eighteen years old! (Funny, aren't women always supposed to be eighteen?? I am thirty-four, of course).

**The Dinner Project**
An aspect of home that I always kept close to me was its food. I miss Syrian food and made it a point to cook it at home. Once, we invited a Welsh lady, Rose, to our house, who loved our food and encouraged us to start making Syrian food professionally. In fact, it was with her support that The Syrian Dinner Project hosted its first community event. This was a huge success and we received positive feedback from everyone who attended it.

The Dinner Project officially began in 2019, right after I gave birth to my son. I run this project along with my mother and another fellow Syrian Rula. Rula had come to Wales from Syria separately, and we met only in Aberystwyth for the first time. While this was off to a great start, the world had other plans. Immediately after we began, the pandemic struck, and it became very difficult for us to manage. It was a challenging time for everyone, and everyone was struggling during this period. In fact, we decided to make food for the NHS workers at Bronglais Hospital in order to support them. We cooked for 120 people at the NHS, and this effort was much appreciated by the community. We just wanted to show them our support for the courageous work that they did for us every day, at risk to their own lives and wellbeing.

The community in Aberystwyth has helped us a lot, and Rose still supports our business. When we had our first in-person event at the Medina restaurant in 2019, there were over a hundred people in attendance. The restaurant space was so beautiful, and we aspire to have a restaurant like that of our own someday. I strongly feel that the people here have always shown up for me, and helped me when I needed help, and I wanted to do something for them. So throughout the pandemic, we delivered food to people's houses from our home. This brought everyone great joy and we kept ourselves busy in an unpredictable time as well.

Making food is something that has always brought me joy. I used to make meals for my family and that is how I showed my love to them back home. The Welsh people also love food, and that is another aspect that brings us together culturally. They express love through sharing food with each other. I love *cawl* in Welsh cuisine, and also the sweet, baked goods that my friends here make for me, such as banana cakes and traditional Christmas desserts. I was even invited for a Christmas dinner one year and I loved the experience. I love sweet food in general, and I make *baklava* for everyone at our pop-up restaurant – a sweet pastry with chopped nuts and honey, and *Yalengy* – a traditional dish made up of stuffed vine leaves. Everyone likes and appreciates our traditional dishes, and this gives me confidence to make more and make better food for the community here.

Wales is a stunning country; there is no doubt that I love living here. Some of our family's favourite places to visit in Wales are the Elan Valley and Devil's Bridge. The views from these locations are absolutely breath-taking, and they never fail to amaze me. On some days, we cannot believe that these places are just waiting for us at our doorstep. I could not have imagined a life like this a few years ago. I do feel at home here in Aberystwyth, but I cannot deny that I also miss my country. I miss being young in my hometown, and I miss my friends. I left my sisters in Egypt, and my brother passed away in Syria. I always think of them and remember them. Of course, I speak to my sisters regularly, but it is not the same. Having said that, Aberystwyth now feels like my second home.

My English-speaking skills are improving by the day, our business is growing, and we have already been recognised by multiple awards in the community – The Nation of Sanctuary Entrepreneur Award; The Food and Drink Award by Menter Aberystwyth; and the Ethnic Minority Welsh Women Achievement Association Award for Self-Development. Most recently, I was given the chance to participate in The Kitchen Cabinet on BBC Radio 4, hosted by Jay Rayner. I was so proud to be given the opportunity to talk about the Syrian Dinner Project and our food on a national level. The future is looking bright today as I feel increasingly settled here and see my children flourish. I also dream of opening my own Syrian restaurant someday, and I am taking firm steps towards realising that dream in the not-so-distant future.

# Floundering in the Darkness

## Miranda Mertha

As a child, I thought about the UK a lot. The UK was that country where people went, and returned after six months to build a mansion in their hometowns in Zimbabwe or buy expensive cars. It was the land of opportunity, where dreams could be manifested. The idea of a land where ordinary people could go and become rich within a short space of time was fascinating. The UK was the dream and everyone who was old enough was either harbouring this dream or then, living it. Those who were either too young or too old, or those who lacked the opportunity, simply existed on the sidelines of the dreamers. If they could not go to the UK themselves (perhaps because they could not afford to), they could still benefit from, and could plan their lives and hopes on, their kinfolk who had already settled in the UK, or on those who could still realise their dream of living in the UK.

I was sixteen years old when I got my chance to come to the UK. I had just finished my GCSEs and was getting ready to either return to school for my A levels, or then go to university. Instead, I found myself at the airport coming to this cold country. My uncle, my mother's brother who lived in the UK at the time with his children and their mother, was the one who invited me. I remember that I was not really taken in by the idea despite the promise that it held. My hesitation was founded on the fact that my father had died about four years earlier, and I did not want to leave my mother.

My mother was a victim of the classic behaviour of extended family members in Zimbabwe, who wanted to strip her of everything my father had left behind. She was at the receiving end of countless family schemes and unwanted advances from men, who would not have dared to look her in the eye when my father was alive. However, through that experience, she found the strength to fight and hold on, and I like to think she derived that strength from our presence.

So, I did not want to come to the UK, but I found out rather quickly that my coming to the UK was not really an invitation. It was a summons, or a command of sorts. The decision to come to the UK was a decision that was made for me 'in my best interest' but I could not see it at the time. However, I wasn't expected to see it for what it was, or even appreciate it. I was expected to obey, and perhaps be grateful. And that is what I did. I came to the UK, but I did not really own that decision as mine.

When I arrived, I found that even though my uncle had invited me and had promised to look out for me, I was on my own. It was my responsibility to navigate life in this new country. I had no one to turn to in order to answer my numerous questions like, 'How do I get a job in this country? Where do I get a National Insurance number? What is a NI number, and who do I speak to about it?' My uncle had done his part. He had facilitated my coming to the UK. By his invitation, he had put me on level ground, and I now had to negotiate the hurdles along the way on my own, like everyone else and make something of myself. I had a life in Zimbabwe and a mother to look after. Consequently, I had to figure out things very quickly because there were people back home who were tailoring their dreams and their lives on my arrival in the UK. The minute I stepped on that plane, it was assumed that I became responsible for my family in Zimbabwe, even though I was a child myself. The feeling of plunging into uncertainty was not just about me not finding a job; it was also about being sorely ill-equipped to adjust to life in the UK and being beholden to the expectations that Zimbabwean society had of me.

I depended on, or rather I should say, I thought I could depend on my peers for much-needed information. However, I am from Zimbabwe, and my people are known for their gatekeeping. Nobody was ready to offer me information. Everyone protected their territories and did not want other people to be better than them. It was sort of like saying, 'I don't want to help you and I am okay watching you flounder in the darkness.' Now that I think about it, it is really sad. It is sad that we are a people who hinge our joy on the failures of others. Since I could not get the information that I needed, I went to college to begin my A levels. Even though the new academic year had already begun, I had a Cambridge certificate for my GCSEs. That was helpful and I did not have conversion issues, and could enrol easily.

After the first year, we had the summer break, after which I returned for the second year. As we resumed, I found out that I had fallen pregnant, at seventeen, without help in this cold and still not wholly familiar country. It is difficult to describe in words the horror that I felt in that moment. I was afraid and confused, yet I was creating a life which I had to be responsible for at a time when I was still to come into my own. Looking back at that time, it feels like I was forced to skip some important milestones in the growing process and just transition directly into a full adult. But the natural process of growing up was not for me; instead, I had to go through it quickly for my child.

After the initial shock, I returned to school and attended as best I could, but the first trimester of my pregnancy was very difficult. I could not concentrate, and I had a ticking clock and a growing stomach that reminded me I had a child coming in a few months and I needed to figure out what I was going to do. In this frame of mind, I finally gave birth to Matthew and found myself in Swansea.

I love Matthew – he is the light that came to brighten the darkness in which I floundered. But his birth came with all sorts of problems. Having fallen pregnant and delivered a baby at seventeen, I became a sort of pariah among my peers. I was considered wayward. It was of no consequence that girls my age were promiscuous and experimenting with sex. Nobody talked about the fact that I chose life for my baby. Instead, I was the one who got pregnant – the wayward one. This sense of displacement affected my relationships with the people around me. They were mostly married people and I was a teenage single mother. I think they regarded me with some suspicion and warned their daughters not to follow in my footsteps. As far as my son was concerned, he was a child who hung out with other children his age. Of course, the nuances were always there and the fact that he had one parent instead of two. But I doubt he was affected by the eyes that both pitied him and questioned his very existence.

My troubles at the time were compounded by the fact that I still had the expectations of my family in Zimbabwe to live up to. If I did not send something home in the form of money or gifts, I could find myself the subject of discussion in a family conference. At the time, I had not yet learnt how to say no to this kind of oppressive expectation. I had to send money to pay my siblings' school fees. The amount of money I had to send increased because the economy had crashed and prices were skyrocketing. I had to pay for everyday items such as uniforms and shoes. Yet, I had a child who had all these needs and no father to support us. He needed shoes, he needed clothes, he needed to be part of the school play and I had to provide for all that. I carried within me a trauma that I didn't even know I was going through. All I know is that I was always the last consideration on my list of priorities.

As is typical of fathers of children born by teenage girls, Matthew's father left. We split up and he went to the United States of America. With regards to child support, I considered the issue quite critically. I realised that I could not put myself through the trouble of trying to obtain child support from him. It was too much work and he was the kind of man who would do everything in his power to make the process difficult for me. So, I let him off the hook. What I did however, was make the decision that Matthew would not have access to his father. I would raise him singlehandedly and make sure that he wanted for nothing. I became his mother and his father.

My son is twenty years old now and we have survived; we have thrived even. What has happened in the course of these twenty years is that I went into a mode where I did not value myself. I was neither the first nor second person on my list of priorities. Somehow, I was able to provide for my son. Somehow, I managed to fulfil the expectations of my family in Zimbabwe and send money to them. But I felt immense anxiety when I tried to spend money on myself. I could not, for a long time, just walk into a shop to buy clothes or shoes for myself. I could not think of myself. I only got the bare essentials that I needed to keep myself going, to raise my son and keep being useful to my family.

As I have matured, I have had to unpack that sense of inadequacy and self-effacement. I have had to re-evaluate my relationship with money and myself and I have arrived at a place of contentment, where I can prioritise myself at times, without feelings of guilt. Indeed, arriving at this point of healing has made me a woman who can be of use to herself and her society.

In 2020, after we emerged from the quietness of the Coronavirus pandemic, I set about becoming the woman that I have always wanted to be. I went to the gym and got in shape. I got a tattoo, acquired a nose ring and became generally more confident in myself. I remember my son asking me repeatedly if everything was alright. He wanted to know if I was going through a midlife crisis that was sparking these changes. Looking back now, undoubtedly I was going through some changes. I had raised my boy, prepared him to leave home – he is a student now at the University of Bristol – and I was turning to myself. I had found my voice, had learnt to say no to black tax, and I became a well-rounded woman.

This also required evaluating my relationship with God. As a younger person, we went to church religiously. My mother would wake us up every morning for prayers and we attended every service. When I came to the UK, I realised that even though I connected with God, I didn't quite know Him. He was my mother's God, who I sang and prayed to because she said so. However, when my troubles began, I felt that my mother's prayers worked. So, I prayed too. In fact, my connection with God is the reason I did not abort my child. I knew that even though I had made one mistake, I could not commit murder (abortion is regarded as murder in Christianity) to sustain my life. So, when my friends were frequenting clubs and I was unable to join them because I had a toddler, I spent the time praying. There was a period of about two or three years when I spent every Saturday night praying for my son.

Becoming a well-rounded woman also meant that I looked at my relationship with independence. I have worked throughout the past twenty two years to make sure that my son does not struggle like I did. I have put resources aside and I stand in my own right. What this means is that I am not dependent upon anyone's charity to live my life. One of the most relevant aspects of my life where this plays out, is my relationships with men. Men generally do not like it when women don't need them. It burnishes their ego when women whine and doll themselves up for them. It so happens that I am not that sort of woman. I enter into a relationship with a readiness to leave if things don't go well. Unfortunately, there are not many men who can handle strong women.

These days, I am a lot of things. I was once in a job that paid me quite well, but I hated it. I remember driving home one day and I asked myself how I got here. That day I realised that everything I had done and everything I had achieved was because I had a child at seventeen. It was as though I was trying to prove to the world that I could do it. It was never about what I really wanted to do. I realised then that I could not live my life in response to a twenty-year-old trauma. So, I stepped out of that job. I rose above that fear and let my passion rule me. I still work a day job which I like, but my real passion is the counselling that I do. I have become the woman who advises mothers on how to raise their children. I can do this because of my lived experience. I was once the girl who needed that help, and I figured it out on my own and with God's help.

I work as a business consultant and a business coach. I work with women from their startup stage as they try to grow their business. My approach to this work is holistic. Sometimes, I ask women about their marriages and about their children, and usually they want to know how that impacts their business. My life's experiences have taught me to approach things from a holistic standpoint. So, if a business executive is not meeting their goals, it could be something in their marriage that is affecting their output. If I understand what is going on, then I know what to expect and we can then get the business on track.

In all of this, my move to Wales has had a significant part to play. They say home is where the heart is and the heart is where I have now planted my roots. Having said that, I am also still close to my family in Zimbabwe. Yes, things have not always been easy. Racism exists here too – even if we cannot touch it, we can feel it. But I strongly believe that it is a matter of perspective. If we take it to heart, we will never be able to achieve what we want to. We need to rise above it.

Today, this is the woman I have become – a single mum who is not yet forty years old, with a twenty-year-old son who is walking beside her in her life's ambitions. I have become the woman who is not just surviving, but thriving. In fact, I am planning to go to Paris with my son to celebrate my fortieth birthday. I am no longer floundering in the darkness, I have found the light.

# A Sari and a Train

## Kate Cleaver

When I was a child we would visit my grandmother, a tiny woman who lived in the front room of my aunt's house. Poorly, she would wave from her bed, her hand and arm skeletal, or she would be sitting in her brown leather TV chair watching the colours of India.

'Come, my girl,' she would say and then give me a toothless kiss.

She smelled of spices and the inexplicable scent of Parma violets. She was not my favourite person. As a child I couldn't understand why she didn't just get up and move, why she lived in a room in my aunt's house and why she couldn't go to the toilet on her own. She was, however, sharp in her mind. I remember watching Bollywood movies and eating Indian sweets with her, but she perplexed me. I am told that in my early years, I used to speak Urdu with her, but now I have no memory of it. I can recall a few words of Swahili, but the memory of the language is shrouded in mist.

Back then, no one knew that I had learning difficulties. It was the seventies and eighties and learning issues were not really considered, especially not in my school. During my school years, I had to deal with bullying for both, the colour of my skin and my learning problems. Now, I have completed my PhD and have been an author for over a decade, but the discrimination I faced has not faded from my memory. On one ill-fated day I remember my classmates, including my friends, lining up and spitting on me. The teachers simply turned away and just 'didn't see'.

My grandmother, of course, knew none of this. She was the matriarch and the centre of my father's family. The world of the

Murrays revolved around her. I however, was confused. She was an enigma to me and any questions I had related to her behaviour, were simply put down to her old age, even though she was, in relative terms, not that old. Life had been difficult for her. I didn't know then, but she was a hero for our family. The reason our family revolved around her, was that there would have been no family without her.

My one regret is that she never appeared to be proud of me or my choices of toys, which included a white, blonde doll. It seemed to me that she considered me the oddest of her grandchildren on account of not knowing or understanding how my brain worked and what I was facing. By the time I had the autism and dyslexia diagnosis she had passed, so she never understood.

My Indian heritage wasn't explicitly talked about. However, now I have made it almost my mission to find out how my father's family came to live in the UK. My grandmother spent her formative years in an orphanage on account of her stepfather disassociating himself with his wife's illegitimate, mixed-heritage daughter. My great grandmother was a nurse in British colonial India and fell in love with an Irish soldier. Even though I always saw my grandmother as Indian, she was also mixed race, like me. Fair of skin with light eyes, she was a beautiful woman. Her biological father was sent back to Ireland and never returned, thus leaving my great grandmother in the almost impossible position of being pregnant with a mixed-race baby that she would have to raise as a single, unmarried mother. As an Indian Catholic, it is very likely that being unmarried and pregnant caused friction in her family and society. She eventually met and married an Indian man, who accepted her, but not her illegitimate daughter. As a result, my grandmother was sent to an orphanage which was also a Catholic boarding school and was separated from her younger half-siblings.

I found a photograph of my grandmother at sixteen, engaged to a man who she probably met in the orphanage itself. The family stories portray this phase of her life as brimming with drama, akin to a dramatic Bollywood film plot. After the engagement, her fiancée left to seek his fortune in Africa and said that he would send for her once he had established himself there.

They were desperately poor, and she owned little. As a result, certain possessions were greatly valued by her, such as any jewellery she owned and the *suphuria*, or family cooking pot. In fact, the whole family has always used the beaten metal cylinders that grace many Indian households, and these have now been passed down to my sister.

While my grandmother was occasionally allowed to see her half-siblings, it was perhaps something that must have been difficult for her, especially in the knowledge that she herself would never be permitted to be fully part of that family. The only option she had, therefore, was to be strong and wait for her betrothed to send for her.

She waited beyond what would be considered reasonable. She made a life for herself. She continued her studies and became a teacher in the same orphanage that she was raised in. Her patience paid off finally, as after five years, she received a telegram from my grandfather informing her that he had arranged and paid for her passage in a ship to Africa.

Her husband-to-be had bought land and was setting up a chicken farm. Nostalgia is a wonderful thing sometimes, for my father, so many decades later, bought a smallholding in Wales and managed to procure the same breed of chickens that he remembered from his childhood years on his parents' chicken farm near the Serengeti. In fact, my aunt and her daughter went back to their childhood home about ten years ago and discovered that their house was now a school.

Faced with the decision to follow her fiancée to Africa, she took the leap. While my grandfather was still not exactly rich, he had secured a job as a printer and enough money to build a comfortable life for his betrothed and any children that they would have.

My aunt remembers the kitchen table in their house in Africa, made from two old doors, with a battered, large pot with an ill-fitting lid, holding all manner of delicious rice, lentils, and curries, which fed not only the family, but also any neighbours and friends who visited. This form of large gathering of family and friends, centring around food is what I also recall from my childhood. Gathering in London to share a bowl of shrimps caught by one uncle and cooked by another, everyone gathering in a garden and laughing in the sun. My grandmother of course was there at these gatherings, silent and watching, lips smeared with oil from the curried chicken. I loved her and loathed her at the same time in equal measure.

Asking questions about her life in Africa and India only resulted in silence. My father's memories of his childhood are limited as he was only a child when they left and moved to the UK in the 1960s. We have some wonderful old photos of him standing in London, pretty much wearing all he owned, and white gloves.

'Why that colour?' I'd asked on seeing the photos.

'Because that was all they had.'

Essentially when they shopped for gloves upon arrival, because they found the UK exceedingly cold after the hot climate of Africa, there was only one colour available – white. The images are stark in their black and white contrast.

My father is one of seven children, the youngest of all the boys. He was born a month premature at a very difficult time. My grandparents' house was ravaged by a grass fire and my grandmother had to give birth to my father in a barn-like structure. Helped by a nun, my father was also baptised immediately as they thought he wouldn't survive, but thankfully, he did.

I went through a phase when I decided to fully embrace my Indian heritage and largely wore Indian attire to fit in. I enjoyed wearing those outfits, but sadly, they only made me stand out even further. My grandmother mainly wore saris, the colours I can only imagine from the old dusty black and white photographs, which depict her as a young, beautiful woman, with a slight smile and mischievous eyes. However, knowing her as I did, only towards the end of her life, I find it difficult to reconcile her early images with the silent and weathered person with paper-thin skin.

My aunt once related an extraordinary story about my grandmother to us. She told us that my grandmother almost lost her two oldest sons. With a laugh and a shake of her head she recalled how my grandmother had gone back to India each time, to give birth to her children. We are British Indians and when partition occurred in 1947, creating Pakistan and India, my family decided they would retain their Indian citizenship. However, my grandmother's family and half-siblings were all in what would become Pakistan, and she wished to see them one last time. The timing could not have been worse. She was all set to get on a train from India to Pakistan, with one of her teenage daughters and her two oldest sons, when she realised that if they left India at that point in time, and went into Pakistan, they would be repatriated as Pakistani citizens. Upon this realisation, she held on to her daughter's hand, but could not locate her sons, who were then probably already on the train. When the train began to move, she was determined to stop the train and retrieve her two sons. My grandmother, that tiny woman, stepped onto the tracks and stopped the train whilst around her there was chaos. My aunt ran onto the train, found her brothers and hauled them out. Our family's story could have been very different if my grandmother had not acted in the way she did. I often wonder at her bravery, and I try to match that woman with the lady who liked Parma violets and Bollywood, who refused to wear her teeth and was living in my aunt's front room.

That woman who stood on the tracks, and the old lady I knew, seem like two different people. She was both, I understand, but by the time I knew her, she seemed to have lost a part of her. Maybe it was the losses as well as the gains that aged her. Both, the emigration from India to Africa and from Africa to the UK, were traumatic. In Africa, their farm near the Serengeti was confiscated as part of the political changes and stirrings within the country, and the land was given to the indigenous population. Life in Africa had become difficult and hence, the decision to move to the UK was made by my family. But the general silence about our family history has left me guessing at so many details and obvious gaps. This has also left me with a strangely dislocated feeling when it comes to where I live. Is Wales home? Or India? Or Africa? I don't know. The trauma of arriving with only a suitcase and white gloves is one I will probably never have to experience, but there is a strange silence when it comes to stories and family history. There was nothing to ground me as I grew. I was a mixed-race child in a world where I was very different, and it left me devoid of personal history. Instead of being proud of the lives my grandmother's and father's generations had led and their journeys, by remaining largely silent, they almost seemed to convey that they were ashamed of it. The stories that I have uncovered though, show that my grandmother was a strong and independent woman, who travelled on her own between Africa and India on several occasions. If I had known the snippets of my history that I know now, when my grandmother was still alive, I would have been extremely proud. Instead, I am left with vague memories and the thought that she found me as perplexing as I found her. She was the reason the family were together. If I could see her now, I would surely try to hear more stories and nuggets of family history, because I have only scraped the surface.

# A Door Opens, and I See My Life Before Me

## Wamagu

**1V.**
A door opens,
And we enter one by one.
We are searched head to toe
As one by one we enter

We must remember all their details,
All the details we want to forget.
Young.
Old.
We sit on the cold long benches,
Wait and wait.

*Come in here*
*Go in there*
*Sit by here*
*Stand by here*
*Do you understand?*

All we need is safety
But.
*Why did you lie?*
Threats
Threats.

All we speak is taped,
Taped and recorded,
One by one.

Some of my experiences are sad, and some of them are good, but
the sum of it all is a story of triumph. Let us begin.

I was born in Kenya, on a farm, so I love the rural life. It trained
me to be tough, quiet, and attentive to the life that could sometimes
be inattentive to me.

This story began when I got married, and my husband was
looking for ways to go abroad. In my country at the time, one
surefire way to go abroad was to go to study. So, my husband
travelled to the US for a master's degree. He left me, a young wife,
to pursue his life's dream. When he completed the course, he
returned to Kenya. However, he had seen a different life from the
one in which we were born and wanted to experience more of the
world; and this time, he wanted me by his side. So, after I had given
birth to one son and was pregnant with another, I followed him to
the UK.

I followed my husband to the UK without any preparation on
my part. I simply upped and followed him because he said so.
Perhaps, I trusted him because he had travelled before and he knew
how things worked in unfamiliar worlds. So, it was not
inconceivable to me that I would be safe and comfortable, and
catered for.

When we arrived in the UK, we found accommodation in a part
of town where there were not many immigrants or people like us.
So, the only person I knew and could relate to, was my husband. I
was lonely, disoriented, and heavily pregnant. I was not pregnant
for long because I gave birth to my second son a few months after
we arrived. So, I was now lonely, disoriented, and mother to a
toddler and a newborn.

Living with my husband was hard. He was a good man, but I had
hardly settled into the marriage when he left to study in America.

When he came back, I had hardly settled into the rhythm of having him around when I fell pregnant. I was nursing a toddler and pregnant again when we moved to the UK. Our marriage had gone through many changes in a short space of time, but we had not yet recovered from the distance created by the separation of his time in the US. It was like we were learning about each other again, this time with two boys in the mix. Unfortunately, I was still struggling with all the variables when my husband wanted us to move again.

I had never been to America. As a result, I did not know what my husband had seen and experienced in the US that made him so dissatisfied with the UK. What I do know is that my husband did not like the UK, and he did not want the children to grow up here. He wanted us to move, but I objected. We were moving around too much. Why, I asked, could we not settle down in one place? My complaint and questioning of his penchant for wanderlust was the beginning of my problems. Our relationship became toxic, our home unsafe, and my husband started abusing me and assaulting me physically. Because of the domestic and physical abuse, I chose to leave with my children.

Raising two boys alone is hard, but it is even more difficult for children to live without one parent. However, there were things to consider. I did not want my children to see me as the victim of abuse at the hands of their father. I did not want my children to have to choose between one or other parent; and I certainly did not want my children to think of their father as a bad person. There is no telling how deeply or how far a child's psyche could be damaged by that. So, for me, the choice was between accompanying my husband in a move to another country, or then raising my boys alone, and attempting to create a safe space for them in which to live and thrive. Whatever decision I took, they would be affected in some way, so I decided to go with the option that included safety for me and a non-toxic environment for them in which to grow. That was how I entered the UK refugee system.

Before I could get into the UK refugee system, I was in and out of court for eight years. I was in court so that I could stay in the UK to raise my sons in a safe and secure environment. My husband offered no support. Instead, he asked me to return the children to him if I could not care for them. Not long after, the Home Office asked him to leave the country, so he returned to Kenya. The last I heard of him, he had taken advantage of some of his connections and gone back to America. We have since, lost touch. I was left to deal with the system on my own. I had no money and I couldn't work. That meant that I had to beg for help, and rely on someone who found a place for my sons and I to live. It was eight years of court appearances, and eight years of running. That's how I came to Swansea.

When I came to Swansea, I joined the asylum programme and had to report at the police station regularly to sign in. It felt as though I, and the other people in the programme, were being criminalised. What had we done that warranted us going to the police station? We asked these questions over and over until somebody finally took up the cause.

Eventually, the court ruled that I be given discretion leave that allowed me to remain in the UK legally for thirty months. However, at the end of the period, I had to pay a sum of money to renew my leave to remain, for my sons and myself at the Home Office. I had to continue renewing our leave to remain permits until I had lived in the UK for ten years. Thankfully, with the granting of leave to remain came the right to work. So, I got a job and earned my own money. Unfortunately, the eight years I had spent earlier between courts were not counted.

In those previous eight years, I volunteered to keep busy. While volunteering at an establishment called the City of Sanctuary, I learned a lot and developed a skill set. While there, I took a human rights course, got my PGCE and got certified as a tutor of English as a Second Language (ESOL). These skills gave me an advantage that allowed me to get a job as soon as I could work legally in the UK.

The story did not become easier after getting the short-term leave to remain. Although that chapter of fear and court appearances had closed, a new chapter of financial deprivation opened. I did get a job immediately, but I had to begin saving a substantial sum of money to pay for the renewal of the leave to remain for my sons and myself. I saved that money from my already inadequate earnings. In addition to the money saved for the Home Office, I paid tax, national insurance, and immigration health surcharge. Then, I paid for basic necessities, such as electricity, heating, transport, and the like. Working also meant that I now bore the weight of time, or the lack of it. I had to plan to get my children to school early and get to work. That kind of life, where there seems to be no end in sight, could drive one to despair.

One day, when I was still new in Swansea, I joined a women's group at the African Community Centre. At one of the meetings, our coordinator, Jenny, gave each of us writing materials and asked us to write poems. Most of us looked at her with the question, 'What shall we write?' I remember that she told us to write about our experiences in life.

Before then, I had never written anything. Growing up on a farm, as children, we were mostly seen and not heard. We were not allowed to speak when the adults were speaking. We hardly spoke to the adults without first being spoken to. As a result, I had a lot of time on my hands and an active imagination that had found no means of release. So, that day, when Jenny asked us to write, it was as though a door opened before me, and I could see my life. So I distilled my life's experiences into a poem. I have now gone on to write a series of poems that I call 'The Door Poems'.

In my poetry, I meditate on my life's choices as a series of doors, behind which I have found rooms and spaces waiting for me. My experiences are the spaces waiting for me behind every door. My choices are the doors that I have opened. There are no choices without consequences in life. Consequences can be good or bad. And I know a thing or two about consequences.

My boys are grown now, and my days of running are over. My older son is twenty-two, but some of the vestiges of those eight years remain. When they were growing and were often on the move, he attended six schools during that period of time. The consequence of that was that my sons could not make friends in school. Every time we moved, they would attend a new school. As is the way with boys, my son would start looking around for someone to attach himself to in a bond of friendship. Learning to rely on, and trust new people in new environments takes time. Usually, and quite unfortunately so, we would have to move soon after my son had identified and made a new friend. My heart breaks even today as I remember his friendship with a Spanish boy in Cardiff. He and the boy cried when I announced that we were moving, yet again, to Swansea. Such emotional turmoil is difficult for a mother to watch. Today, my son is cautious with people. I perceive that he finds it difficult to attach himself to people and commit himself to solid connections and I can understand that. Perhaps, his memories of his formative years linger, and he is still unable to fully accept and believe that he may no longer have to relocate unless he wants to move.

My boys remember. Due to the fact that I was almost always broke, my boys got used to being denied things they asked for – I simply did not have the money. Then, they stopped asking altogether, because they knew we could not afford it. I think it is because they did not want to be a bother. That, in itself, disturbs me. It means they shed their innocence quickly, learning to carry a weight of awareness that must have been too heavy for their young shoulders.

Today, I do not see them asking me for much. However, any mother knows that willingness to help her offspring is as natural as the ability to draw God's breath. More painfully, it seems as though they are afraid of ownership, of building a life, because they feel like they are not allowed to do so. I am afraid that they may not demand much of the world around them or lay claim to a space in which to stand and make an impact. I hope and pray with all my heart that this changes.

My body also sometimes feels the impact of my life's experiences. Having been married before, being a single woman is hard. There have been times in the last fifteen years when my body has hungered for a man's loving touch, the warmth of companionship, and resultant feeling of stability and security. But I remember that I loved a man once; I followed him to this country, and he betrayed me. Would I open up myself to that kind of hurt once again? So, I have fought those feelings and suppressed these thoughts. I still experience low moments, cold, lonely nights, and sometimes my mind cooperates with my body to betray me, but I am still here, and still standing. My faith has been an anchor, helping me view things positively and cope with whatever is missing.

The doors I have opened have not all been gloomy. Some of them have been bright. As I look back, I see that some of my experiences have prepared me for the life and opportunities I have now. I have worked with people in similar circumstances like myself, so I am able to empathise with them and look for ways to help them realise that it is possible to make a successful journey. At the moment, I work for the Health Board. We have an outreach that supports ethnic minorities looking for access to healthcare. Our focus in this programme is to promote health and wellness. Also, I use my knowledge in Food and Nutrition to teach community feeding and healthy lifestyle, which reduces the need for hospital visits.

Now, I hold a regular social event, which is an opportunity for women to come together, share their experiences and find friendship. I do this because I know that things would have been easier for me if I had a support group while I was suffering domestic violence or while I was on the move for those eight years.

Recently, I have started holding a similar social event for men. The space that I have created allows men to come together to speak out, thereby breaking the barrier of silence and internal turmoil that so many men carry within. Men do not like showing their emotions because of a tacit code that vulnerability makes them less masculine.

The results of these social events have been manifold. The relaxed atmosphere makes room for release and friendship. It also creates space for people to have sorely needed information. From my experience, one could be in trouble if one is new to a place and does not understand how the system works, what one can access and how, or what one's rights are. One could find that it takes a long time to settle down. But if one has support, settling down is far easier, as is gaining confidence and pursuing goals. This also helps people to become a positive influence on the community. Many of our women have gone into volunteering. That warms my heart because volunteering is a great way to learn the skills that are needed to survive in this country.

As I found my footing, I have had other doors open to me too. I have had the opportunity to speak and be an inspiration during a refugee week event. Perhaps, I might move towards full advocacy in the future.

Talking of doors, I sometimes think about the doors that I might open tomorrow. For me, faith is a reality: a breathing, living thing. Along with faith is hope. I apply faith to my future, and I hope that it will be brighter than the gloom of the past and the present light that I see.

This is my story: some of my experiences are sad, and some are good, but the sum of it all is a triumph. I challenge you to begin.

# Around Wales with My Heart in My Hands

## Chinyere Chukwudi-Okeh

When I packed my bags and boarded the British Airways flight to Heathrow and then the National Express to Swansea, I didn't imagine how my life would turn out. I missed home all through the journey and thoughts of my children became a heavy burden on my chest. It was the longest journey of my life. As a writer in Nigeria, the dream had always been to weigh my creativity internationally, travel around the world and allow the many twists and turns of this journey colour my writing. The choice of studying Creative Writing at Swansea University was both a dream and a ticket to a new life for my family. As a mother of three, my husband and I deliberately create and dream dreams that would accommodate our children. This was a joint agreement. If the dream doesn't make room for the entire family, then it is not for us. I always paint a safer clime where we could be together with fewer odds. Hence, on my drawing board, I had drawn up our lives in Swansea before making the decision to be the forerunner who would travel first and create room for the rest of the family to join me. The UK Study Route was the most appealing choice.

I felt the deep pangs of nostalgia while settling in Swansea and wanted to be home with my loved ones, my sisters, brothers, parents, husband, and children. In the days to come, I would coil up under the blanket in my tiny cubicle, watching videos and pictures of family moments. My only consolation was the fact that my family would be joining me soon. And the thought of their visas being granted, and their flight tickets purchased, became a soothing balm for the loneliness and aloneness I felt while navigating life in Swansea. But the travel itself was soon plagued by the news that Nigeria had been added to the red list countries during the COVID-19 pandemic, and as such, we would have to pay an exorbitant amount to quarantine in a government-designated hotel. When this happened, I wondered why it seemed like uncertainty had come for a feast in my household. I worried why every victory and glimmer of hope had to be clouded by the possibility of not materialising.

I wished to hold my world in my hands, and play out my outcomes predictably like a game of chess. The joy I felt when I heard the news that the visas had arrived, literally hung like a bubble in the air with this new COVID restriction. We had tangible evidence in hand, but our pockets did not align with the demands of Nigeria's new travel status. Nonetheless, hope, they say, is a waking dream and I believed so much in speaking to God, to the heavens, to the universe. If there was anything Nigeria and my parents taught me, it is to pray as though my life depended on it. Prayer for us in Nigeria is the opium of the hopeless, and the confidence of the oppressed. And when life squeezes the juice out of our dreams and plans, we kneel and pray to the creator who controls life's outcomes. I knew life could change in a blink, and miracles were for tomorrows. So, I called my husband and told him confidently that the ban would be lifted before their travel date. I was vehement, and anyone listening to me would think I had spoken with Boris Johnson and consulted members of the British Parliament. I remember saying by way of a joke, 'Omicron has got nothing on us!' And true to my faith, the ban was lifted two days prior to their flight schedule. I then proclaimed, 'Come 24th December, 2022, we will be together!' The thing about joy is that it comes in the morning and this time it came like a gust of wind.

It happened that the ban was lifted a few days before the travel date but what I failed to mention to my family was the fact that I had wandered and meandered through the slippery slopes of Swansea, walking into all the letting agencies on Walter Road,

Clydach, Uplands and Morriston, and had found no accommodation for us. They were literally coming to Wales to live in a house that I was yet to find and pay for. There seemed to be a thing with Swansea landlords and children. The house would allow a family, but by that they meant a couple without children. No smoking. No pets. No children. And the few that would allow children would only let houses to people with the maximum capacity to pay rent. Curiously, by the very appearance of me, I fit the profile of those who could not pay rent. They probably saw poverty written on my forehead – never mind that I was well-employed. The deception called looks!

'We will put in a word for you. Hopefully, the landlord will consider you,' they all assured me.

There was a particular case in which sixteen contenders had viewed the house before it was my turn to do so. Viewing suddenly felt like being served a buffet but never getting a chance to dig in and eat your fill. I got rejection mails and in some cases I wasn't even dignified with a formal rejection; the agents simply went awol.

There was perhaps a problem with the simplicity of my appearance. In Nigeria, I had the luxury of being called attractive because I had a lighter shade of skin. I am a fair-complexioned black woman. So, it felt good to be called *Oyibo Pepper, Bekee, Nwanyiocha, Omo Pupa Rondo-Rondo, Aponbepore, Yellow Pawpaw* and *Onyeocha*. These were beautiful names for a light-skinned person in Nigeria, and I basked in the admiration that came with being admired in such a manner, never mind that I sometimes felt fat and un-beautiful. But I came to a rude awakening during my search for a house in Swansea. I couldn't help but notice the reluctance to be taken seriously by letting agents. There was an unspoken assumption hanging in every enquiry across most of the letting companies.

There were stereotypes of an inherent inability to pay rent by the very virtue of my colour and appearance – the very colour that many women back home would covet and go as far as using toning and lightening creams to achieve. I had walked into one of the letting offices, and the young man behind the glass quickly rushed to meet me at the door saying, 'Sorry we have nothing for anyone that is not working. We only book viewings for people who are working and can pay rent.' I felt bruised, turned around and started walking out, but the rebel in me couldn't stomach the punch, so I quickly walked back to confront him.

'Please, do you by any chance have a mirror?' I asked.

'Ummm yes. But what do you need that for?' He asked, staring, with a smirk on his face.

'I need to see if it is written anywhere on my forehead that I am jobless. Your hasty conclusion of my inability to pay rent must have been visible on my forehead,' I said and walked out, leaving his dry mouth hanging open.

Some days, I would approach anyone carrying a box or bags, demanding to know if they were moving out of their apartment as I would love to move in. After days of failure, I realised that my family and I would have to return to my tiny room in the attic of some student Chambers in Maritime Quarters to regroup and re-strategise. Desperation defies the parameters of natural thinking. I called everyone I knew, infusing my house hunt in every conversation, at work, in school, in my writing, and at the hostel. And somehow, a couple who were moving out of their studio apartment offered to introduce me to their landlord and letting agent. We wanted a makeshift, or perhaps a temporary accommodation arrangement, pending finding something better.

The thing about my breakthroughs in Swansea was the fact that once I solved one problem, another one reared its ugly head. Can a family of five; a father, mother, two sons, and a daughter, live in a studio apartment? For lack of a better option, we decided to spend Christmas together in the studio apartment and split up after the quarantine period. I paid the rent and bond for the studio apartment a day before my family's arrival, at a price that could have gotten me a flat or house at the time. I worked my night job while simultaneously sorting out the formalities and moved in on the morning of my family's arrival.

My challenges advanced alongside my studies at Swansea University. I wrote my portfolio and reflective essays while fighting these hydra-headed challenges. My nightmares and daydreams became muses for my academic submissions to the Creative Writing Department of Swansea University. I would sometimes write on my phone while in transit and then stay up at night trying to piece together my disjointed and scattered thoughts. But at the end, they managed to come together to form a whole.

In the studio apartment, there was only one bed and no room for a reading table or additional bed. While my three children slept on the bed, their parents embraced the cold floor. And in all of this, I could not but romanticise my football-pitch-sized living room and master bedroom in Nigeria, and how my children would run from end to end, just being children. I compared it to the fragility of our makeshift home and how we walked on eggshells to keep the peace in the neighbourhood.

My husband's lateral flow result came back positive twice even though there were no visible symptoms to back up these medical results. We literally held our hearts in our hands and remained indoors peering through the blinds while awaiting a negative result. We gave him space, as best we could, owing to the outcome of his test. That means we were together but not exactly together as we maintained a long-distance interaction with him, in the same house! One of the gifts of living right off the road is the chance to be next to life, to motion. Life itself becomes your view, the sights, sounds, and movements, a rare gift, and a constant reminder that against all odds, you are still alive, a part of unfolding moving history. As my husband clung close to the blinds, just staring at the road mostly, the children and I busied ourselves with reading and chores.

I had imagined taking my children to the Winter Wonderland for New Year since we would be in quarantine during Christmas. I had resisted the urge to go to the Winter Wonderland and be lost in all the exciting rides before this. I wanted us to do this together as a family but that never happened. Then my husband was selected for interviews, being an accountant and a tax consultant, but his experience and certifications while impressive, were too Nigerian to land him a befitting job in the UK. So, he embraced the support jobs instead. Our house problems persisted as I had to inform the letting agent and landlord about the number of occupants owing to our inability to achieve a split. My sincerity and openness became the beginning of a harrowing journey. A journey that took me to housing options, community centres, Citizens Advice and lots more. My husband and I intensified our house hunt, moving from the pillars of Walter Road, to the post of Morriston and Clydach. We finally settled for a house in shambles! Yes, in shambles! At least we met it in disarray but were promised that work would soon be finished, and it would come out sparkling new.

## And the roof came crumbling down

There is a proverb in native Nigerian parlance that a bird in hand is worth a thousand in the bush. This house with all its shambles and disarray became our treasured bird in hand as the hope of its renewal and redemption through thorough overhauling and painting, became our hope. We got the permission of our new agents and landlord to inform our current impatient and disgruntled agents that our move was near and they could now hold their horses and retreat from their threat. The threat was that we would one day come home and realise we have been locked out and the locks changed. I studied the real estate laws in Swansea which offered some protection somewhat, but nonetheless, I was more restless than the owners of the current house to move and breathe freely in a new and befitting living space. I wanted my three children to have their own rooms and space, just like in Nigeria. So, we began a second phase of waiting for our prospective home to be made homely enough for us to move. This was our longest wait; days turned into weeks as our discomfort increased.

When we moved into this house, it came with mixed feelings. We knew we deserved better as everything looked like it was hanging precariously. First it was an old house, and to add to that, it had an eerie ambience of a house on the verge of caving in. The staircase groaned with every movement of our feet, and some of the doors creaked, as though balanced on very rusted hinges, which they were. The kitchen cabinets were old and outdated and there were no white goods in the house. There was no extractor fan, no cooking set, no fridge, no washing machine and of course the heating system didn't function for days after we moved in. We had to buy a makeshift manual heater from one of the shops and the entire family assembled into one room to share each other's warmth and the artificial heat from this single heater. The toilet had congealed excrement for which the owner of the house had provided us with bleach to clean it. Then the bathroom sink hole was just an empty hole with no drain holes or any drain at all; just a wide gaping hole. It was the peak of winter and the house inside felt as cold, and sometimes even colder than the temperature outside.

For months we continued scraping the toilets and at each attempt, dried faecal matter was flushed down. Soon we realised the carpets and every other thing in the house was hurriedly and poorly assembled to have us move into the house. We had survived one house, but we became quite certain that we had moved into a rebranded problem. We also worried about the garden outside which was heavily overgrown and needed urgent attention. There were piles of debris from the shabby clearing done in order to have us move in, which was cleared by the owner of the house. I have always believed from years of listening to native wisdom from my village of Mbaise in Imo State Nigeria, and from my years growing up in Onitsha, Anambra State in Nigeria, that home is a place we leave in one place, and it welcomes us in another. But looking for a homely place in Swansea to call home became a harrowing journey for us. Home became the warmth we generated for each other as a family, against the cold walls of our immediate surrounding and the outer world.

As days turned into weeks, the walls developed damp and it became even colder. And as weeks became months, tiny black spots of mould and mildew began to spread. We ended up buying mould and mildew removal kits bi-weekly and cleaned like our lives depended on it. My children were badly affected with tonsillitis, respiratory infection, and suspected asthma. Gradually, the weak gum/glue that weakly held together the fragile wood and carpets of the house began to give way as did the rusted hinges of the cabinets, which began falling away.

And then it finally happened, an averted tragedy. We had spotted a well-painted crack line on the ceiling when we moved in. We took a snapshot and notified the landlady and she said she had taken note of it. But on this bright, fateful day, we had gathered in the living room watching a Netflix Nigerian movie. My husband and my first child then went into the kitchen to get a glass of water. As soon as my son got up from his seat and had barely gotten to the door, the ceiling caved in onto his seat as the rest of us ran to the door watching, as the ceiling fell along the crack line earlier spotted.

We immediately notified the landlady, but she simply said she would contact her builder. Moments later she sent a message to say that the builder was of the opinion that my children pushed the ceiling down as they must have been jumping upstairs. This was similar to the response we received when we complained of the mould and mildew. She had blamed us for causing the mould. We later realised that the mildew and mould from the past was painted over and the more we cleaned, the more the stains from the past infestation surfaced from beneath the coatings over it. We waited for months for the ceiling to be repaired. We cleaned and cleared up the broken concrete from the old ceiling ourselves. We avoided that portion of the living room and also avoided the room above it. We insisted on a reduced rent owing to the fact that the room upstairs and part of the living room were uninhabitable. Soon we began the count down to the next improved house as our house hunt began again. Looking for a place to call home became an albatross hanging around our necks, an unpleasant constant in our journey.

During our stay in this house, we continued to receive all the post for the previous resident, which, after a while, became worrying. However, we discovered that the previous resident of the house was an elderly lady who had passed away, which allayed some of our worries. Gradually, home became a metaphor of everything that should be, but hadn't been thus far. Just like the piles of mail we had received for the previous resident, our expectations and anxieties also piled up. The rejections from house viewings also piled up, but our resolve and hopes of moving into a new home were equally as high as the many negatives. And joy was closer every new morning.

I walked around Swansea with my heart in my hands, feeling a certain kind of restlessness and uneasiness; that feeling of being neither here nor there, an exilic consciousness that betrayed the initial joy felt on reuniting with my family. There were 'wow' moments, and these came largely from being completely absorbed in creativity. Every time I channel my melancholy into writing, painting in words what my eyes see and my body feels, drawing my emotions on paper like paint on a canvas, I feel a certain kind of newness. I come alive. However, that which gave me joy was also transient, as it could neither pay my bills nor put food on the table. Hence, my passion often took a backseat as my survival occupied the driver seat. I worked in the third sector, at night and at the weekends, I indulged my passion by writing and taking up opportunities that helped me remain relevant through my creativity. Wales and indeed Swansea has blessed me with tales of a lifetime, but it has also taught me lessons, humbled me and equipped me for the future. I am a better woman, a better writer, a better human being. I have become bolder as Swansea has become my muse. I know the future is bright and there will be many more roads to walk, hurdles to jump over, and challenges to surmount, but I am more equipped. As I continue to explore all my possibilities in Wales, opening up myself and creativity to diverse expressions, I do so with my heart in my hands. All around Wales, with my fragile heart in my hands...

# BBC 2: Proud to be Chinese

## Suzanne Sau San Chung

*Hello and welcome to BBC2.*

*Next up we have coverage from the 14th London International Competition for Traditional Tai Chi Chuan.*

Thus goes the introduction on the BBC before a sporting event. This introduction often begins with a thirty-second countdown accompanied by a soundtrack of orchestral music, flashes of images that show athletes competing in various categories. The music builds up the viewer's anticipation while showing authentic footage from the BBC's archives. As the timer winds down to zero, you will often get a broadcaster beginning the TV programme with the words above or a variant of it. The BBC introduction shows that one of the best ways to start something good is by declaring your credentials. For the BBC, their credibility is bound up in their name. A name serves as a reminder of an entity's essence to those who already know; and as an introduction to newcomers. I am proud to be reporting on BBC2, and proud of myself.

My name is Suzanne Chung, and my BBC credentials are not of that revered broadcasting corporation. I am a British-Born Chinese (BBC); and am the younger, second non-identical twin. BBC1, my older twin sister, had a nine-minute head start before my own awkward breach debut. So I guess you could say I was someone who was already very familiar with drama, even before I entered that world.

My parents were living and working in Canada when my mother became pregnant with me and my sister. Understandably, she was terribly anxious about having twins, and flew to Scotland to see my *Por-por* and *Gong-gong* – my maternal grandmother and grandfather, for emotional support. That was how we – two bonnie wee Scottish lassies – were born! Soon after, we flew to Hong Kong to be looked after by my *Ma-ma* – my paternal grandmother. The Chinese have specific terms by which we address, ascertain and distinguish gendered relationships i.e. maternal or paternal grandparents for instance, unlike English, which tends to be less specific and more generic where gendered relationships are concerned.

Depending on who you ask, you would be told that we stayed in Hong Kong until my sister and I were one or three years old. We then emigrated to Canada, because that was where my parents were working – my father owned a restaurant there. In Canada, we learned the English language using flashcards which had pictures and English words on them, along with Chinese characters. We had to learn English this way because we had no English-speaking neighbours in Hong Kong. I can still remember learning the alphabet sitting at iconic desks, which I was surprised to see, can still be purchased online. We attended ESL (English as a Second Language) classes in school. My sister and I conversed in Cantonese in school when we did not want anyone to know what we were saying. Looking back, I guess it was certainly beneficial to keep practising Cantonese outside of the home.

In parallel, even to this day, I still try to improve my traditional and simplified Chinese language skills while using the social media platform, WeChat. I also actively try to use colloquial Cantonese when I communicate with other Cantonese-speaking friends. My father used to point out the traditional Chinese character for a word when I typed the simplified version. But in general, it is so much easier to learn and remember characters with fewer strokes. For my job at the Chinese in Wales Association (CIWA), I am encouraged to type in simplified Chinese, as the majority of service users cannot read traditional Chinese. So, it is a struggle to try and learn both forms of written Chinese. However, as a person of Chinese origin, I feel it is my innate responsibility to learn both forms of Chinese. For those interested, I also use the Pleco app to learn some Mandarin slang/lingo. As a child, I used to love watching Chinese TV channels to learn simple, repeated Chinese characters from the subtitles. My favourites were Wuxia and Chinese Kung fu series and movies. Wuxia is a genre of Chinese fiction featuring travelling warriors of ancient China, often depicted as capable of performing superhuman feats of martial arts with very ornate clothing. These TV series and other popular Jackie Chan films formed the bulk of my favourite viewing while growing up, and this also helped to improve my Chinese language skills.

As an ethnic Chinese person growing up abroad, a certain amount of discrimination was almost expected, despite the fact that Canada was often proudly described as a 'melting pot' for different cultures. When I moved back to Scotland when I was eleven however, I found that I was not only discriminated against for belonging to another ethnic origin, but also for all the Canadian traits, accent, and jargon that was obviously part of everyday life in Canada. It is often the case that people tend to be averse to things they do not understand or cannot identify with. However, I faced flak from my classmates in school because I used words differently – for instance, instead of 'full stop', I said 'period'. In short, my most mundane use of North American terminology became the cause of bullying by my classmates. It was a learning experience for me to discover that one person's normal is a novelty for another person. Despite this, I feel my life experiences and various incidents where I was discriminated against, have made me into a stronger person. They have not deterred me from accepting my heritage, but have driven me to be an advocate for it. I have even gone as far as learning Mandarin, and using it to learn Tai Chi and Qigong from martial arts masters; something that had always fascinated me as a child.

Today, people still comment on my English, whether it is my Canadian twang, or simply surprised that I, a Chinese person, can speak English so well. My accent has been influenced by my formative years in Canada and Scotland. My mother's English is akin to what is colloquially known as 'Chinglish' with a liberal injection of a Glaswegian twang and in my aunt's case (she lives in Swansea), her English accent is influenced by the Swansea twang. Personally, I prefer speaking with my mother in Cantonese as that feels more true to who we are, our roots, origin, and culture. I find it amusing that people are often shocked that I speak English so well, and even in this day and age of apparent knowledge of the world and exposure to various countries and their cultures, they still think that every Chinese person they encounter was born in China. Also, once when spelling my surname out using the NATO phonetic alphabet, someone even made a comment saying 'Oh, they even taught them that!' I noted it, but did not respond to it in order to be polite. But of course, I was taught the same as everyone else. Why are they so surprised when my English does not even have a Chinese accent to it? However, I do believe that being Chinese and living abroad has resulted in me amassing different life experiences than if I had been born and raised in China. Our experiences and terms of reference are undoubtedly different, and they form part of who we are.

Apart from being Chinese, another thing that has defined my experiences is that I am a twin. My sister and I were born in the Chinese year of the tiger and are both Scorpios. So, we both have very strong personalities. Although we are not identical, we are very similar. Therefore, people often mistake us for each other. I was once at the receiving end of an accusation in my first weeks at university. A new friend said I had snubbed her when she tried to say hello. It turned out that she had met my sister and mistook her for me. When we met up at her house party, she finally realised that I really am a twin. Something similar happened when an ex-colleague had moved offices and they had bumped into my sister in the elevator.

Even when we were back in Canada, a classmate had said I made her cry during recess/break time when I hadn't even left the classroom. My twin sister and I have therefore been inextricably linked with each other's lives, even apart from the natural sibling bond we share. My sister is proud of my achievements, attributes, and talents, be it my interest in various crafts, photography or then the martial arts, the latter being the thing that people most associate with me.

My mother's younger sister lives in Swansea and we loved visiting her and her family during our Easter holidays, when we resided in Scotland. My aunt had always mentioned to me that the Welsh people, and especially those in Swansea, were very welcoming towards Chinese people, as well as those of other ethnicities. Also, my boyfriend (now fiancée), was from Swansea. I had tried and failed to find a suitable job in Hong Kong after completing my studies and the cost of living was far higher in Edinburgh (if I had decided to continue living in Edinburgh) than it was in Swansea. Therefore, all of these factors drew me to Swansea as I prepared to enter the next phase of my life. Once in Swansea, I not only became involved in the Chinese in Wales Association, but also the Confucius Institute. Through these two organisations, I was able to pursue my cultural interests, meet other Mandarin and Cantonese-speaking people, including Chinese students and make new friends. I feel entirely accepted in Wales and love being part of this vibrant cultural exchange. I do not necessarily discern the nationality or ethnicity of my friends as Welsh or otherwise – all I know is that I love meeting new people and forging new friendships.

I have been settled in Swansea now for almost fourteen years. During this time I had also integrated into the Chinese in Wales Association (CIWA) as a volunteer. Swansea is kinder to Chinese people and perhaps other nationalities than other places I have lived. As a City of Sanctuary, Swansea has opened its arms to people of all nationalities; we all thrive here. This kindness has allowed me to become my authentic self and explore my interests. Living in Swansea has also allowed me access to scenic surroundings, where I can pursue my interest in astrophotography. Six years ago, I started learning Tai Chi at CIWA. It was there that I met my Tai Chi and Qigong soul sister. I was translating Mandarin instructions to her and we immediately bonded. She then introduced me to Master Faye Li-Yip. Through my hard work and determination, I had learned Tai Chi and Qigong from Master Faye, a true martial arts master coming from a martial arts family lineage. Through Master Faye's online Zoom classes, I have learned so much and have thrived. I feel a great sense of accomplishment for receiving two medals at the London International Competition for Tai Chi Chuan and Qigong in 2022 and 2023. I am now studying for a Duan 2 Diploma from the International Health Qigong Federation, and will be doing a Tai Chi and Qigong instructor course next year. There is much to be excited about. I also had the opportunity to write an article for the International Tai Chi and Qigong Federation in their December 2022 Newsletter about my Tai Chi and Qigong journey.

It was back in Scotland during my teenage years that I began inculcating my interest in various arts and crafts, while simultaneously helping out in my father's Chinese takeaway restaurant. I continue to share my interest in these arts and crafts with my community even today. I hope to inspire others to learn about, and also love the Chinese culture that I am so proud to be a part of.

Presently, I work at CIWA as a youth worker. I work towards the wellbeing of the local Chinese community and their youths. My work is part of the HarMindise project, where I effectively act as a bridge, connecting youths from various ethnicities to Chinese culture. It is my way of making sure that our culture, even for those in the diaspora, does not die out.

British-born, Hong-Kong/Canada/Scotland-raised, and thriving in Swansea, I have chosen to promote my Chinese heritage. I do so by adding a Chinese flavour to all my arts and crafts, and by sharing my Tai Chi and Qigong learning. My various influences have given me a richer and fuller experience as I promote my Chinese heritage. While remaining steadfast in advocating my Chinese heritage, I am also keen to incorporate the various influences that have shaped me, be it in Hong Kong, Canada, Scotland, or now, Wales. I have even considered giving my future child a Welsh name. A friend once suggested that I should start a blog to share what it was like to be a Chinese girl growing up in Britain. In this way, I could use the platform to showcase how my Chinese heritage melds into my British heritage. An elderly community member said that all my skills are like a set of knives, suggesting that I am a talented Jack of All Trades. Chinese community members as well as friends boost my confidence and encourage me in my endeavours, especially my promotion of Chinese culture and heritage.

I return now to my opening acronym and why I choose to associate with it. BBC2 shares programmes of depth and substance. In my opinion, it has the greatest range of knowledge building programming of any BBC television channel, paired with distinctive comedy, drama and arts programming. In parallel, just like the channel BBC2, I somewhat identify with what this broadcasting channel represents. I, also BBC2, encompass a wide range of experiences and an all-round character. I have grown by merging all the places that I come from, along with all the interests that I have picked up along the way, as well as all the skills that I have developed and the opportunities that I have come across; and I have arrived here, where I thrive. Therefore, I have developed an identity of my own, and discovered my best self. I am a Chinese woman born in Scotland; and raised in Hong Kong, Canada, and the UK. I am like a prism encasing all my experiences; and my journey is like the white light passing through the right conditions, giving birth to glorious colours. Some people say 'We never know the beauty of the rainbow unless we see it'. I hope to share this beautiful and vibrant rainbow with the world.

# Once Somewhere in the Middle East, Now Swansea

## Monica

**1.**

My country in the Middle East is the land of many wonders (I shall withhold the name because it is a small world out there). It is a land where rich history mingles with sumptuous cuisine, whose aroma reaches around great mosques with intricate architecture. It is the land of wonderful people with hearts as large as anyone could imagine and compassion as deep as the lowest points of the ocean. It is where I was born, raised, and planned my future. It is also the place that I had to leave in a hurry, leaving behind little pieces of me to show that I was once there, once loved, once dreamed, once gave, and was given to, once just lived.

I was in my second year of Pre-med (Biology) at the university when politics came and interrupted our lives. We left our lives behind. My father left his job and everything he had built with his sweat and tears; I left my preparation for medical school entrance exams; my siblings left friends, school competitions and their well-imagined plans for the future; my mother left her mother. We left all this and more, and we fled. Despite fleeing, there were things we could not leave behind – our heritage, looks, heart and love for our homeland.

When we first got here, we felt overcome. We had nothing and knew no one and we did not fit in. We had only a vast expanse of emptiness before us and could hardly make sense of this new experience. Back home, we had urgency, a purpose to our lives and our basic needs were met. Here, basic needs became the purpose that we sought urgently amidst excruciating loneliness. Even though I had my family around me, I was lonely. Unfortunately, everyone in my family was lonely. Thankfully, those early days did not last. We clawed our way out of that despondency into the British refugee system and found reason and urgency to live again.

I was soon in a position to go back to school. I tried to get into medical school here, but my two years as a pre-medical student back home did not count. Like most universities in my homeland, my university adopted the American education system, and it was not adaptable to the British system. I, too, did not want to lose two years of my studies. Then there was the other issue of money. As refugees, we could not work. The adults in my family received £50 every week to cover basic expenses. Needless to say, our basic costs were not covered. Being a refugee, I could not be treated like a home student. I had no access to scholarships, grants or subventions that could make my journey easier.

The first thing I did was resolve my career problems. I wanted to pursue medicine, but it seemed like becoming a doctor was no longer proving to be feasible. It seemed like that was another ambition I had left behind when I fled. So, after some time, I opted for Clinical Psychology. As a clinical psychologist, I would be able to help people. I would work with a psychiatrist to make people better in their minds, mould their behaviour and pull them from the brink if the need should ever arise.

The next step was to solve the problem of fees. In order to raise money for school, I began talking to everyone who would listen, in and out of the university, until I found someone ready to give me a loan with the understanding that I would pay it back after graduation. However, fees were only a part of my worries. As a university student, I needed books and I needed to be able to go to university every day. I could not do that on £50 a week. Nevertheless, I tried and began my university journey.

My first year as a student in Clinical Psychology at the University of Swansea soon ended. I received my grades, and I was on a first-class track. Although I was happy about my grades, I know I had not been at my best in that past year. There were other things occupying my soul. The space and peace of mind that I could have devoted towards greater excellence were occupied by the anxiety that we were not fully settled here. We were aliens, unstable and incomplete. We could have been whisked off to another part of the country at any time. We could have been sent back home to the Middle East at any time. We had not got Leave to Remain in the UK. The fear of being sent back home was real. It was real because the reason we left the country in haste was still present. Added to the anxiety was the need to survive, and that was difficult.

Thankfully, we now have received our Leave to Remain. We can now officially live and work in the UK. That means I can work now for as long as I need to get what I need and focus on my studies. That also means that we no longer risk being sent back to the Middle East.

## 2.

One would think that for a family that had gone through so much, we would lean on one another and find strength. Unfortunately, we did not. Everyone in my family had their own pain, and we were all trying our best to stand upright. We were connected to each other, and we also affected each other. What this meant was that if one person was down, everyone felt down. If one person had an emotional struggle, we all had emotional struggles. If one person complained about racism or how some random stranger questioned his right to exist as someone from the Middle East in the UK, it was all our senses of self and location on the line. If one person was sick, it was as though we all needed a doctor. So, to safeguard one another, we each kept our pain private and tried to deal with it in the ways we knew best. In the times when it was impossible to keep private, each one tried to minimise the effect of their troubles on the rest of the family. The family was already going through a lot.

We were not free to return home; yet, we had not been able to fully integrate properly into society. We were barely eating well, and our dreams were somewhat on hold. We did not love one another less; we just showed that love in a rather peculiar way. Some might even call it tough love.

3.

My mother's body is turning on itself. She has a disease that has an impact on her immune system, attacking her tissues and organs. This auto-immune disease is difficult to diagnose because its symptoms mimic many other diseases. Depending on the severity of the disease, the kidneys, joints, or body systems, such as the digestive or respiratory systems, could be affected. The scariest thing about this disease is that it has no cure. There is no one day to look forward to when you can be free of this disease. Instead, there are only good days with the disease and some not-so-good days.

Due to the disease, and compounded by the weather, my mother has some problems with her joints. Therefore, mobility is a bit difficult. I think about what else my mother could be going through that she is not telling us. How does one live fully knowing that one's body can run amok without a moment's notice? Why does the body choose to betray its owner when her world has fallen apart and is just getting rebuilt brick by brick? Why, in God's name, do things fall out of balance?

My mother is a strong woman. Despite the disease, she is now at college full-time studying English to communicate better and even teach it as a second language. In her free time and in the summer, she volunteers at a large refugee programme. She interacts with new refugees to get their stories so that they can be settled in properly. This interaction also helps the refugees to be calm and trusting of the new country where they have arrived after having survived trouble at home and a sometimes long, arduous journey. Most importantly, my mother's work as a volunteer gives her purpose. For every person she interacts with, she also comes away with a breath of fresh air. At home, we were not lazy people sitting still and twiddling our thumbs. So, if this is our new home, we must make the best of it despite personal challenges.

### 4.

One of my brothers got into trouble at school over a game of ping-pong. Ping-pong is a popular game in my home country, and my brother is a proficient player. His skills are excellent and almost as good as international competitors. One day, at school, my brother played ping-pong with a group of boys. Owing to his skills, he defeated some of the boys. One of the boys started to issue invectives and he called my brother derogatory and racist names. But my brother kept quiet and won again. One boy, in particular, threatened to hit him on the head with a bat. But my brother was undeterred and won the next game. So, the boy broke the bat on my brother's head. My brother would not have it, so he defended himself. Needless to say, matters came to a head in the form of a fight, and the school authorities got involved. My brother was to be punished because he should not have defended himself on school grounds. What was expected of him was to have called a teacher and reported the matter. I think the school is right about these rules. If everyone were to fight in self-defence, society would simply descend into anarchy. My brother accepted the punishment. He had defended his honour as a young man on and off the ping-pong table and would accept the consequences like a man. However, he said the boy who instigated the altercation had to be punished too.

I have considered this situation and have a few thoughts. I do not think the boys were bothered that they lost the game. I think they were bothered that they lost the game to a boy from a different country. It is quite interesting that success and defeat have to be calibrated according to skin colour. In this case, sportsmanship did not work because race was involved.

To return to this story, the other boy did not accept the verdict of the school and would not serve the punishment. The boy told his father, and more threats were issued. The school advised us to go to the police.

The police told us that they could do nothing because what had happened simply involved verbal threats. They would spring to action when something real – like a physical action – happened. For some reason incomprehensible to me, having a ping-pong bat broken on my brother's head does not quite count as physical action, just like my two years of pre-med studies back home did not count for university here. I find it concerning that the police would not take a racist threat seriously; that they would rather investigate a crime than prevent one. I do not know if it is because the other boy is white and my brother is a refugee, or if the police are just inept. Perhaps, the reason is not any of these. Whatever it is, it is not good. What they are proposing is like giving potent medicine to a sick man after his breath has left him.

My brother moved cautiously after that incident. He and we do not want to find out how efficient, or otherwise, the police investigation system is. We don't want to know how race and refugee status affect the dynamics of these investigations. Prevention is better than cure.

## 5.
I remember clearly when we first came to Swansea. We arrived in Swansea in the middle of the school year. My youngest brother could not attend school immediately because all the schools close by were full. When he was finally given a place, it was in a school further away. My brother could not handle the transport system independently, and we had no money to pay for his regular commute. However, the biggest problem was that my brother was afraid, and we could not let him live like that. We took the matter up with a regional counsellor, who listened to our appeal and let my brother enrol in a school nearby. Even then, he walks to school in the company of an older brother or me to deter bullies.

In school, my brother did not get a sports team to join because all the teams had been formed. Thankfully, he has developed a bit of resilience since then. Sometimes, knowing the place we left behind, why we left it and what exactly we left behind, helps in developing that resilience.

## 6.

Things are getting better. We are being integrated in our community here in Swansea. Swansea particularly is a great place to nurture diversity and growth. I am learning to give back to this country that let us in when our home forced us out. We are going out more. The other day, we went to Cardiff as a family, enjoyed a movie night, went karting and generally had fun. We are beginning to laugh a lot more now. We are regaining a sense of who we are as a family.

Recently, my mother asked me to go out more, to meet new people and make friends. So, I did. At the African Community Centre, I met a friend and colleague who directed and encouraged me and soon, I unfurled and started to dream. I wanted to make an impact and influence change and positive action through my own experiences. The result of that dream was a project through which we encourage women, especially asylum seekers and refugees, to project beyond their challenges and circumstances, towards a better and brighter future. It was necessary to prepare young girls for life after asylum and refugee status and bequeath them with the prerequisite skills for the future of their dreams.

This project also encourages women to take risks and stretch beyond the stereotypes prescribed by society for women. We encourage women to desire the best life, pursue the most extraordinary excellence and reach the loftiest heights in business, entrepreneurship and other aspects of life. I have support, and things are looking up.

I like the air in Swansea; I can breathe deeply. It felt like I started breathing deeply again after we got our Leave to Remain. With that breath came release; with that release came a clear sight to look out to the future.

Maybe one day we will return to our country in the Middle East. I do hope that one day we can go back. Going back, however, would require that the thing that chased us out of the country has tired itself out or no longer exists. When that day comes, we will find ways to contribute to the homeland. Until that day comes, we will make the most of the life we have here with all its gifts, peace, and beauty we have received.

# The Art of Movement:
# Bringing Anime to Wales

**Eiko Meredith**

Japanese by birth, I grew up in Hiroshima – instantly known as the unfortunate target of the first atomic bomb in 1945, and less so for its Peace Memorial (a UNESCO Heritage site) and its Flower Festival and the International Animation Festival in its successful post-war reconstruction guise. My father was an English teacher in school (later promoted to Professor at University), which aided my English language skills throughout my school and university years. As a child however, I suffered from asthma, and I stayed indoors much of the time upon doctors' advice. I did eventually outgrow the asthma but staying inside encouraged me to watch Anime and read books/Manga comics, which is my passion. By the time I was at university, my love of animation/anime had spurred me on to get involved with the Hiroshima International Animation Festival to the point that I then, naively, imagined that I could perhaps organise a similar event on a professional level, not just as a keen amateur.

I used to frequent a small cinema that was, at the time, located at Hiroshima Station, which usually showed international/independent films. One of the films screened there was *Wallace and Gromit*, prior to its subsequent global popularity. In fact, I was one of only three people in the audience. This sparked my eager interest in, yet another form of animation i.e. clay animation.

By this point, I knew that I had to at least try and further my interest in a more focused direction, which would aid me in going down a more professional path of animation in some capacity in the future. After studying at Hiroshima City University, I stumbled across an animation course in Bristol, which helped me to learn more about stop-motion animation.

After the course I met my future ex-husband, and in 2008, I moved to Wales after getting married. I can say now that I am extremely happily divorced. In the interim however, I managed to establish the first annual Japanese Animation Festival in Wales, known as the Kotatsu Japanese Animation Festival which has now, I am pleased to say, been extended to Aberystwyth and Bangor.

The first year of the festival took place in 2010 when Chapter, the Arts Centre and home to art-house cinema in Cardiff, had just been refurbished, and was on the look-out for new and diverse events and ventures. They kindly embraced my proposal of pioneering the first Japanese Animation Festival in Wales at that venue. The weather unfortunately went against us that first year and our first festival was shrouded in heavy snow and inconvenient conditions. This meant that the festival's full potential and impact could not be realised in that first year. Fortune was on our side however, as Chapter asked us to organise another festival the following year and the rest, as they say, is history.

Prior to attending the animation course in Bristol, I had been to the UK on a few occasions with my parents on holiday, but I found that there was a vast difference between visiting the UK on holiday and living in the UK for an extended period of time. The first thing I struggled to get used to was the rainy weather, something that many Japanese people find difficult to acclimatise to. Another stark difference between Japan and Wales in particular, was the work ethic. In Japan, if someone is asked to do something, it will be done straight away, because of a strong emphasis on efficiency, whereas I found that if I requested someone to get something done here in my immediate surroundings in Wales, it had to be followed up a few times before the matter was attended to. It might be due to people being busy, but I find that the attitude at the workplace, in comparison with Japan, is far more lax. Sometimes, this is also a positive thing, for the work ethic in Japan can bring with it a high level of pressure, stress, and anxiety. Consequently, work pressures and stress over here are not at the same level as they are in Japan.

The language and accent of Welsh people also took a bit of getting used to for me at the beginning. I found that in Bristol, the spoken English accent adopted a flatter tone, whereas in Wales, it is a lilting accent and at times, I feel that the Welsh people speak much faster too. In a short space of time therefore, I had to adapt to the cultural, language differences between Japan and the UK. It has been a learning curve and took a long time for me to figure it out. Many kind people helped me and that was needed especially as I have to survive in this country, after divorce, following an unhappy marriage.

Working to establish and promote the Kotatsu Anime Festival kept me going during that difficult time, and it has been a very positive aspect of my life in Wales since I moved here. In general, I feel that the people in Wales are friendly, empathetic, and helpful and in particular, everyone associated with the festival has the same interests as me and are interested in Japan and Japanese culture. Our working relationships therefore are bolstered by this thread of common enthusiasm and appreciation for the artform and its country of origin.

We experience some difficulties such as limited funding, as all the cultural organisations face. We do not receive any funding from the Welsh government. Instead, we depend on funding from some Welsh organisations as well as the Japan Foundation London, and our sponsors. We have to work within these parameters and limitations, which is not always easy if you would like to bring more directors and host more Q and A sessions and Workshops. Forging collaborations with the Aberystwyth Arts Cinema as well as Pontio in Bangor has proved to be popular. Most universities now tend to have their own Anime Societies and our festival in both towns becomes the focus of these societies as well as providing other local enthusiasts access to enjoy Anime on their doorsteps.

While I do still visit Japan from time to time, I feel like Wales is my home now. I met so many lovely people here, especially through the festival. I also think that I am fortunate because in general, especially when compared to other nationalities, people here tend to be fascinated by Japanese people, their culture and most importantly for me, Japanese films and Anime/Manga. Therefore, I rarely faced any sort of discriminatory remarks or behaviour in all my years in Wales. In fact, I feel a bit of a misfit in Japan now. Sadly, there appears to be certain tacit norms and rules of decorum, dress and behaviour which places additional pressures on women in Japan especially. They are expected to follow the same fashion trend for instance and in general, feel the pressure not to stand out as non-conformist. In Japanese we have a saying that roughly translates as 'the long nail will get hit'. Even today, it appears that the gender imbalance is not resolved despite Japan's obvious advancement and progress on so many other fronts. In Wales, I have observed many more women in charge and there is certainly a more understanding environment for working mothers. The gender inequality is also evident in the Anime industry as the majority of the animated feature films are directed by men. As a result, we use the F Rated system (https://f-rated.org/) which was founded by Holly Tarquini, a logo used for the female driven films that are directed/screen-written by women.

The aim of our festival is to not only show good quality diverse Japanese animated films, but also introduce a more gender-balanced dimension. Sadly, it is not easy even today; still, we do our best.

In Japan, once women have their own families and children, it becomes very difficult for them to continue and further their careers in animation because of the working conditions.

A director and the founder of an animation studio Usagi Ou, Yuji Umoto (https://usagiou.net/) in Japan is currently trying to encourage more women to come back to work after having children. I sincerely hope more can be done in the future to ensure anyone can work for the Animation industry regardless of gender or care responsibilities.

My love of Japanese Animation is a common thread that has run through my formative years in Japan to present day. One of the main reasons I decided to establish the film festival in Cardiff was that in 2010 (unlike now with the numerous streaming platforms), there was still quite a long lag between the release of Japanese films, especially Animated films and their availability in the UK. Setting up the Japanese Animation film festival meant that not only I, but also all Anime fans in Wales could have access to the new films screened in a cinema near them without travelling far. Apart from my family and friends, there is little else I truly miss about Japan – perhaps the food? I made a conscious decision not to dwell on what I left behind in Japan when I moved to Wales because I regarded it as pointless. The decision to stay here was mine and therefore, there was no point in harking back on how things are done in Japan. Maybe some Japanese people still act in that way but not me.

'Try to live with what you've got' was my motto. In general, my personality is an adaptive one and I feel like I would be able to live contentedly anywhere. Many of my friends here are Welsh and that is down to our common love of films and animation (not only Japanese ones). As time has gone by, my comfort levels with life in Wales and sense of integration has steadily increased.

There are many castles in Wales which, funnily enough, resonate with my life in Hiroshima. We have Hiroshima castle in the city and even though I am now thousands of miles from my hometown, there are gentle associations and connections that still seem to link me to my city of origin.

Lastly, if my experiences can be an inspiration to other women or aid other people – any gender – who are in an unhappy situation as I was, then I will be more than happy to tell my story. If you would like to do something, no matter how big or small, just do it. There are always people who are kind enough to help and support you to achieve what you really want to do in your life. Sincerely I hope my story provides the means for achieving positive outcomes for anyone, especially other women.

# From Cat City to 'the fort on the River Taff'

## Anum Munawar

Kuching, popularly known as 'Cat City' in Malaysia. This was the only home I knew until I was sixteen. Historically, it had been part of the Bruneian Empire and had been occupied by the Japanese during World War II, but mercifully escaped destruction. It was and still is, the capital of Sarawak, which is today, part of Malaysia. Apart from its quirky Museum of Cats, it is also a gastronomic hub, recognised by UNESCO. These are just some of the intriguing, and at times, endearing facts about Kuching, but for me, it was my home.

As it happened, the kindergarten I attended was the same one my mother taught in, but I progressed to an all-girls primary school, when my awareness of myself and as it turned out, my life experiences began evolving. At the age of six, I was diagnosed with macular degeneration (a condition that I had been born with) and the slow decline in my vision commenced. I lost my central vision at the age of eight but still maintain my peripheral vision. Prior to the age of six, I had already developed photophobia and dealing with sunlight or bright lights was a problem. I also had difficulty in recognising colours despite my mother trying to teach me the various colours. Since I was colourblind, I used to loathe and fear art classes in school as I found it impossible to identify appropriate colours for painting. Therefore, when I finally lost my central vision at the age of eight, I had already been dealing with visual problems. Nevertheless, it was a difficult phase for an eight-year-old girl who could not quite comprehend why she suddenly could not see distant objects, for instance. If there was such a thing as a silver lining in a situation such as this, then it was that the resilience of youth and limited understanding of the world around us and lack of maturity at that tender age, saw me through the period of adjustment. Having already dealt with a range of visual problems prior to losing my central vision, the eventual loss of it was something that became that little bit easier to get used to. Today, looking back, I feel fortunate that I lost my sight at such an early age. It allowed me to adapt more efficiently and quickly to, and come to terms with, my altered circumstances. I always feel that it is far more traumatic for people who lose their sight in their later years as they often have to relearn how to live with sight loss, whereas adapting to sight loss in phases was part and parcel of my formative years, and living with sight loss was for the main part, the only thing I knew.

Unfortunately, my impairment became the cause of the appalling manner in which some of my teachers treated me, something which today would be tantamount to bullying and discriminatory behaviour. It is quite telling when I think back on those years and realise that in primary school, the only bullying I was subjected to was by my teachers and not my peers. In secondary school however, it was the other way round. I did also have to contend with discrimination by one teacher who consistently pointed out the likelihood of my school years amounting to very little due to my impairment. To add insult to injury, the teachers never failed to compare my academic achievements with those of my older sister, who also attended the same school. My sister was a straight A student, whereas I struggled to keep up on account of the lack of accessible aids, assistance or even consideration shown by my teachers and peers.

Matters came to a head when I underperformed in the State Examinations. My mother expressed her displeasure at this by going away to her family in Pakistan for six months and not speaking to me for the duration of her stay there. Her reaction affected me greatly. To add to this (I was thirteen at the time), I had also got sick and tired of everyone telling me that I would not be able to do anything with my life. I had reached the end of my tether. I consciously decided to channel my energy, long hours, sweat and tears into focusing on not only keeping on track with academic work, but also excel in it – and I did! I gradually rose up the class ranks and by the time I was in my GCSE year (the equivalent of GCSE in Malaysia), I was at the top of my class and found that I had become one of the most popular girls in school. My success came on the back of much bullying and a lot of hard work.

A certain incident will always be engrained on my brain. One of the teachers who seemed to have it in for me throughout secondary school, made it a point to erase the lesson on the white board quickly, thereby not giving me enough time to copy it. I began borrowing notebooks from my classmates in order to complete copying the lessons. However, this came at a price – literally, as I used to give them my lunch money of five Ringgit each time to borrow their books. This same teacher once noticed that I had borrowed my classmate's book to copy the notes. She snatched the book from me, brought me in front of the whole class and proceeded to denigrate me, saying that I was useless and so blind that I should not have ever been sent to a mainstream school. I could never succeed academically and did not deserve to be in that school. I ended up sobbing in front of the whole class and remained upset all day. In theory, it could have been an incident that could have scarred me indelibly, but I got my retribution two days later, when I topped the Maths exam and later that year, received the Best Student award. According to Michelle Obama, 'When they go low, we go high'! My mother was with me when I received the award and she said that she did not even need to do anything to rectify matters with regards to the teacher's obnoxious behaviour – the universe had done it all for me. She did, however, chide the teacher later on that day for bringing students down instead of encouraging them and boosting their confidence and morale. She went on by saying that I am strong and can fight back, but such behaviour could destroy somebody else who isn't. I hadn't realised then just how upsetting this entire incident had been as at the time, I had a fire inside to succeed no matter what and prove everyone wrong. But in hindsight, I recall the impact it had on me. It pushed me to succeed throughout my life – perhaps I should be thanking her!

Difficulties on the academic front however, persisted despite the good grades I achieved at the GCSE level. My mother relentlessly made enquiries at various colleges in order to procure A level admissions for me, but this time round, I was turned down, not account of my academic results (which more than met the requirements), but rather, on account of my disability. This cemented the family's decision to send me to Cardiff, where, by this time, my older sister was settled with her husband. With much trepidation, I began the next phase in my life in a country and city that I had never visited before, and was not familiar with in the least. Even though I was living with my sister, she was far too busy setting up her own endeavours to provide the practical help that I could have benefitted from at the time. I could not depend on her or my brother-in-law to find my feet in my new, albeit a bit rainy environment. There was also much catching up to do. I had arrived in Cardiff in December 2006 and consequently had missed an entire term of the first year of my A levels. My sister insisted that I had to sit the Maths Core 1 exam within eleven days of my arrival. As if hitting the ground running was not daunting enough, my academically driven sister insisted that I had to obtain nothing lower than at least 90 per cent. All my initial intentions of going sight-seeing upon arrival and enjoy my first Christmas season in the UK, melted away. It was worth it in the end because I maxed the exam!

I was enrolled in an external school in Cardiff, but benefitted greatly from the home tutoring that my sister was qualified for, for students sitting their A Levels. It is akin to home schooling and I was one of her group of students. Unfortunately, the negative experience of bullying seemed to haunt me even in my new environment, and at the hands of my new peers and continued until

I went to university.

It took a while for me to find my way in the city. My sight then was good enough to read bus numbers and explore the city and its streets on my own, but it was a difficult phase – I missed my mother. I was able to call her only sporadically because calls to Malaysia were extremely expensive at the time. Every experience has its implications – this one, I suppose, allowed me to become a little more self-reliant at a critical time.

I tried to immerse myself in many of the opportunities that my fellow students availed of. One such endeavour was the Duke of Edinburgh training, for which I eventually successfully completed the silver medal level, but not without hardship and some fear. A couple of the members of the group that I was with were downright mean. I remember going through a field of horses and we had specifically been told not to make any sudden or loud noises. One of the people in the group knew that I would be the slowest due to my impairment and he made a loud noise after everyone else had got to the other side, but while I was still negotiating my way through the field. During the same trip, we were crossing a path over a river and even though he knew I could not swim, he pushed me into the water. I managed to hold onto a hanging branch and pulled myself out. Back then, while the supervisor would be looking out for everyone's safety, we could not really complain about anyone or anything unless something had gone terribly wrong. After all, the objective of these trips is perseverance and endurance. It is a different matter altogether when the absolute need to display endurance is a result of deliberate and vindictive actions at the hands of a peer. I am glad and relieved to say that things are a bit different now on Duke of Edinburgh trips. Consequently though, I absolutely refused to progress further on to the Gold Award level of the Duke of Edinburgh training.

The beginning of the best years of my academic life started in 2008. I began my Pharmacy degree at Cardiff University. Looking back though, perhaps I should have broken out of Cardiff and chosen

Bath University, where I had also been accepted. Nevertheless, I have no regrets. I created strong bonds of friendship and for the first time, was free of bullying. The workload was great, but I knew I had to work hard to succeed. I was on a student visa and if I had failed, I would have had to return to Malaysia, where I would never have had the same academic opportunities. I trained for a year after graduating with a degree in Pharmacy and became a qualified and practising Pharmacist from 2013 until 2019. This too came with its own challenges. I had initially always wanted to do Medicine, but due to my impairment, even if I had studied Medicine, the Medical Council would not have been able to register me as a practising doctor. It was devastating when I realised that I would not be able to pursue the career that I had wanted to since the age of twelve (I had been passionate about helping people), but Pharmacy was my next best option since the Pharmaceutical Council agreed to register me as a Pharmacist once I graduated. Happily, my working life was enjoyable and I was still helping people and making a difference and felt rewarded. In 2019 though, I lost more of my sight and took the very difficult decision to step down from practising pharmacy. My manager had been exceedingly encouraging and happy with my work and was upset with my decision. However, I felt that safety of the people I would be serving came first. I constantly worried about making a mistake with prescriptions due to my limited sight, which could have implications on the lives of others. This potential burden of responsibility was not one I was prepared to carry. If I had harmed someone with my mistake, I would never have been able to live with myself. At the same time, I felt like I was leaving behind a part of me when I left practising pharmacy.

Coincidentally, in September 2019, I had an invitation to attend a volunteer event for all those volunteering with RNIB (The Royal National Institute of Blind People), for whom I had begun volunteering while I was still at university. I met the then RNIB Community Connect Coordinator for Wales, who encouraged me to volunteer more actively. I soon set up a Bollywood dance group which gave me the opportunity to pursue another passion of mine i.e. Bollywood dancing. Simultaneously, we set up another group of visually impaired Muslim women in Wales, and we called it Women with Vision. It was a phone group as the members lived in various parts of Wales, but the main aim was to talk with, learn from and encourage each other. Unfortunately, soon after, we had to face the biggest challenge in our lifetimes – the COVID pandemic. This however, meant that our phone group, meeting once a month, became even more crucial to those living through lockdown, lack of social contact and isolation.

Directly connected to one of the primary aims of this anthology, I procured a job working for Diverse Cymru, through which I set up several support groups aiding refugees and asylum seekers to settle into their new environments and begin assimilating and integrating. Meeting them was a huge eye-opener. I met several women who had gone through numerous hardships to get to the UK. Learning about their difficult journeys and experiences made me appreciate my journey and life. It was extremely fulfilling to help the people I encountered with the methods of aid and support that we had at our disposal at Diverse Cymru, and watch them take their first steps forward, even if it was baby steps.

While my stint at Diverse Cymru was highly rewarding, it was dependent on funding and therefore temporary. Fortune struck again and I heard of a job vacancy in RNIB for the post of Community Connection Coordinator for Wales – I applied for it and was successful! The biggest relief was that it was a permanent job, thereby ensuring financial independence and security alongside work that I am passionate about. It does keep me very busy, constantly liaising with RNIB volunteers who facilitate a wide range of phone or in-person groups consisting of registered blind or partially sighted individuals, providing one-on-one support to people struggling with sight loss and organising and running creative events for volunteers and members of RNIB.

Here is my life to date, but was life in Wales a culture shock for me when I first arrived? Undoubtedly! Coming from a tropical climate in Malaysia, it took an age to acclimatise. I missed my mum's cooking and the food in Kuching in general, and found myself losing weight initially. I had been used to extremely spicy food, but find that now my palate has adapted to the more mellow flavours in the UK and my spice tolerance has decreased; something I lament. But my education in the culture in Wales also occurred simultaneously. I not only got into the spirit of Easter and Christmas, but also learned about Guy Fawkes Day and Bonfire Night, an incident that I had hitherto been clueless about. I was also schooled in Welsh history and culture by a good friend, who is a native Welsh speaker. She tried her utmost to teach me a little Welsh, but eventually ended up learning more Hindi and Malay from me than I learned Welsh. The cultural exchange also continued through the Bollywood dance classes that I used to run via RNIB in 2019. I truly believe that absorbing the culture of the country in which one is living and simultaneously imparting a little of one's own culture to the people around us, is a significant part of integrating and assimilating. More often than not, if we are willing to understand another person's culture, that person is also keen to understand ours. We learn from each other and consequently, broaden our horizons – this, in my opinion can only have a productive outcome.

This aside, I was positively basking in the confidence and independence that living in Cardiff had bestowed upon me. I was accepted for who I was, despite my sight condition. It was easy to make friends who did not focus on my visual impairment, but rather recognised me for who I am. I had experienced none of this in Malaysia. Here, I get on with my daily life without focusing on the fact that I am disabled, whereas in Malaysia, I felt that I was made to feel disabled.

I came into a sort of family set-up when I first arrived in Cardiff, living with my sister and brother-in-law. Sure, they were busy with their own lives, so much so that we never really celebrated Eid or birthdays together. In fact, I celebrated Eid and birthdays with my friends at university for the first time since arriving in Cardiff. I did miss the vibrancy and lively atmosphere of celebrations back in Kuching in my initial years living with my sister and brother-in-law. Nevertheless, they were my safety net and support system.

Ironically however, Cardiff also reminded me a little of Kuching. Both are relatively small, comparatively quieter cities, people are friendlier than they are in London and consequently, having got my bearings in Cardiff, I can navigate my way blindfolded – just as well, given my deteriorating eyesight. Would I ever consider going back to live in Kuching though? Never. I would never have the same level of independence or opportunities that I have been fortunate enough to avail of in Cardiff. I have lived in Cardiff now for more than half my life and it is my home now – I feel I am half Welsh now.

# Zambia and Wales – The Longing for Home

**Osanna Peters**

I was born in the land of the Zambezi and The Congo rivers; a land of plateaus and river valleys, a land that is in the landlocked heart of Africa – Zambia. I grew up in a newly independent Zambia, after it had gained its independence from British colonial rule in 1964, when Northern Rhodesia became Zambia. While the vestiges of colonial rule still lingered in the form of the commonly spoken English language for instance, the soothing familiarity and warmth of its indigenous tropical climate and the sights, sounds and smells of my childhood in my homeland have been an integral part of me, even after over three decades of living in Wales.

Most of my family still lives in Zambia. Even though some of them married foreigners, they preferred to settle down in Zambia, as there is a certain unique appeal about that country. With low humidity levels and plenty of sun, the weather strikes the right balance and for me, it is a kind of Paradise. There are ten different languages and about eighty different dialects spoken in Zambia. Ironically, since it was a British colony, what unites the languages is English, for English is spoken in most places. Often when people visit Zambia, they want to stay and never leave. This is the effect the country has on visitors. I am one of the few members of my family who left as I fell in love with an Englishman and moved to Wales.

I had lived in England for a while in earlier years in order to study for my A levels, but I had never lived in the UK for an extended period of time. I had considered England to be a fun place, but that was only in the context of my education for, I soon returned home once my education was completed. After meeting my husband however, and being taken to Wales, it was a very different experience altogether, as Wales seemed like a completely different country. I had always been a city girl. When I was studying in London, I used to work and live around Sloane Square and Knightsbridge, in and amongst all the buzz of the capital. Suddenly, I found myself in the middle of nowhere in the heart of Wales.

We settled in the village of Llangadog in Carmarthenshire. In fact, I got married in Wales two villages away from Llangadog, in a village named Llanddeusant in the Black Mountains of the Brecon Beacons. I think the inhabitants did not know what hit them as I had so many of my family visiting in order to attend my wedding and suddenly, there were numerous Africans all around – it was a very African affair!

Having said that, I was extremely touched by the manner in which the villagers incorporated Welsh traditions into our wedding day. A loud gunshot woke me at dawn on my wedding day. When I gazed out of the window, I saw the local dairy farmer who had performed this ritual, with the explicit intention of driving out all the evil spirits from the area for our special day. Later, as we left the church and got into the car to drive away, the villagers came out with flowers in hand, and tied a rope in front of our car. We then had to throw coins in front, and only then did they allow us to pass. This was another Welsh custom. These warm gestures on their part and joyous atmosphere, made me feel truly part of the community on that day, and made my special day even more memorable.

Since Llangadog is a village, we often had to drive to larger towns to avail of amenities such as dental practices. My dental practice was in the town of Ystradgynlais, a word that initially sounded like gibberish to me, especially given its spelling. If one is not familiar with the Welsh alphabet, reading Welsh words is a challenge as Welsh words are often difficult to get one's head around the pronunciation. Moreover, the drive from Llangadog to

Ystradgynlais takes us over the mountains, which are largely brown and devoid of the lushness and vibrancy of the green vegetation that abounds on some of the other Welsh mountain ranges. In my mind, it seemed like the wilderness and I often asked God what I had done that He banished me to the wilderness to live. Later on in life, when I pondered over this question, I reasoned that living in an environment that seemed like the wilderness enabled me to discover the person that I am today. In Zambian culture, one is never an individual – one is always part of a family. The family structure is very strong – parental influence and the influence of siblings, and extended family members is dominant. Our thoughts are often never really our own. The family is all-encompassing and it is all about who we are as a family. Each family member is a reflection and representative of that all-important family. In Llangadog, it was quite the opposite. In general, the culture here is a much more individualistic one in my experience, and each person is encouraged to become their own person. I too acquired my own individuality after coming to live in Wales, and developed my own personality and character.

However, there wasn't that closeness that is a hallmark of Zambian culture and initially, I used to feel rather lonely because of it. In the beginning, I used to keenly miss my life in Zambia with family all around, and neighbours and friends dropping by for a cup of tea at any time. The day could never be planned by us, as it was often planned for us. Things gradually began shifting for me thereafter. The Welsh lifestyle and culture that I had not initially taken to, began endearing itself to me as I realised the benefits of my new lifestyle and the new culture that surrounded me. I started realising who I was and what I represented without my Zambian family around me. I gradually found that optimum balance but that took many years to achieve.

To allay some of that initial loneliness, I joined a literature class. I was the only black person there as the group was overwhelmingly Welsh and white. However, I also soon realised that the main issue that Welsh people had in some cases, was not with black people like me, but rather English people, such as my husband. I was accepted from the start. I have now lived in Wales for about thirty-four years and when I first arrived, I was the only black person for about the vicinity of ten villages around me. I used to joke that I could never run away from home because it would be easy for people to spot me in the area as the only black person around. Similarly, I always had to watch my actions, for people knew me and recognised me. I never experienced any racist behaviour. People never treated me differently – they were always kind and friendly. Having said this however, my daughter did have quite an unpleasant experience in her school when she was about six years old. Another child refused to play with her on account of the fact that she was black and this experience did affect her for a while.

I keenly felt the lack of a social life in my early years in Llangadog. The farming community in the area especially, were not as social as I had hoped. Even if I invited them to my home, the invitation was never reciprocated, even though they were always happy to accept my invitation. When I expressed my puzzlement over this, my Welsh friends explained to me that inviting people over for dinner parties to their homes for instance, was not part of the common custom. In Llangadog, due to the nature of the largely farming community, which kept to themselves mostly, I did not feel very welcomed, but as I learned later, that was not on account of who I was, but rather the way of things in that area. I did often wonder that if I had faced an actual emergency, would anyone have even been aware of that fact? Such was the level of isolation and lack of interaction amongst the inhabitants in Llangadog. It therefore took a long time for me to adjust to the way of life and culture that was prevalent there.

As I broadened my horizons and began making friends in the nearby town of Llandeilo, the situation was different. There, it was more of a professional community with academics and media personages. There, invitations were readily issued and reciprocated.

Yet, it was more common to meet outside in a restaurant for instance, than at each other's homes, which was unlike the practice in Zambia where it is common to be invited to people's homes. I then wondered if this was the case in Wales because, unlike Zambia, there is no help at home and hosts would have to do all the preparations and cooking themselves. As a result, it is probably often easier to meet in a café or restaurant. These were some of the dynamics that I had to deal with initially, which did leave me with strong feelings of loneliness.

I tried to combat some of the feelings of isolation by getting involved in some of the events that take place in and around Llandeilo. Llandeilo is fast becoming a trendy town with poetry and literature festivals as well as a Jazz festival. Apart from that, it also has a lovely Christmas fair in the run up to Christmas and while I am not involved in the organisation of these events, I enjoy participating in them. Now that I have lived in Wales for so many decades, I feel like I have established my own social group here. However, although I have a strong group of around six friends, most of them are from Europe or England, apart from a Welsh friend, who is part of the media and is known beyond the Welsh border. Most of my close friends tend to be exposed to a more international way of life. Therefore, in my experience, making friends with core, native Welsh people has been quite difficult. Even during COVID, I did not feel the kind of community spirit and togetherness that seemed to be prevalent in so many other areas.

Apart from friendships and close interactions, I thoroughly missed the food, the comfort of *Nshima* and relish, the festivals and the social environment back home in Zambia. The weather in Wales was also a huge challenge for me to overcome in the beginning. In Zambia, when it rained during the rainy season, people tend to stay indoors if they do not have to go out whereas here, since it rains most of the time, we have to simply get on with it despite the rain. This also required a period of adjustment, as did overcoming the darkness of the cold, long winter nights. January and February are still difficult months of the year for me because I tend to slide into a depressed frame of mind. As far as it is possible, I tend to make sure that I am out of the UK, usually back home in Zambia, during this time of year. I return to Zambia at least once a year and sometimes twice a year. My children also used to accompany me on my trips back home.

By profession, I am an entrepreneur. My husband used to run team-building workshops for large companies such as Shell, etc. In due course, we also decided to branch into running holiday lets and we have visitors from all over the world. Even though I made Wales my home over the years, I still consider Zambia my true home. I miss the comforting warmth of the sun, the light, the garden, and the unique sounds of the environment in which I grew up. I long for that familiarity. I feel like my body is in Wales but my heart is in Zambia. In short, I long for all that I had to give up when I moved to Wales. The idea now is to spend three months of the year in Zambia and nine months in Llandeilo – the best of both worlds.

# A Tale of Three Continents

## Naheed Kaderbhai

**Jalandar** – 1920s pre-independent, pre-partition India. A young man is sent to Mombasa in the British crown colony of Kenya, as a surveyor for the railways, working under the British. Soon he is joined by his wife, and they initially settle in Mombasa. The couple are blessed with a daughter and two sons. The young man soon moves up the ranks and begins training other surveyors for the British railways in Kenya. He goes on to be awarded with an MBE for his work with the railways and the Indian civil service in Africa. That young man and his wife were my grandparents and their daughter, born in 1928 in Mombasa, was my mother.

**Aligarh University** – 1942 India. Another intelligent, young man, pursuing his higher education at one of the best universities in India, becomes a chaperone for his sister who was travelling by ship to Mombasa to join her husband. He does not return to Aligarh to complete his studies. He meets a young woman in Mombasa, they get married, and he also joins the Civil Service. They move to Nairobi. This young couple were my parents. My siblings and I therefore, were born in Nairobi.

My father continued working as part of the Indian Civil Service in Kenya until his resignation. He was asked to train a white civil servant, who would be placed on a higher position in the white Civil Service in Kenya. My father objected to this on the grounds that he was as qualified as the person he was training and therefore, should also be considered for the higher post. However, due to racial and ethnic discriminations and power dynamics, my father could never be included in the white Civil Service at a post that he was qualified for. On a matter of principle then, he, along with a Sikh and Hindu colleague, resigned from the British Civil Service in Kenya.

My parents, while strongly instilling in us our Indian heritage as well as clear consciousness of our African environment, were egalitarian and secular and imbibed the very same notions in their children. We grew up with peers from various ethnicities and religious leanings and spoke Swahili, Hindi, Gujarati, and Punjabi, along with English, which was the medium through which we obtained our education. We were Indian and African.

When I was thirteen, my parents left Kenya and we moved to Uganda, which is where my father obtained a job with a transport company. It was in Uganda that we, as British citizens due to my father's previous position in the British Civil Service, saw our educational avenues narrow. First preference for A level (the Ugandan equivalent) and university seats was given to Ugandan citizens over British passport holders like us.

**England** – late 1960s in the wake of Enoch Powell's 'Rivers of Blood' speech criticising the rates of immigration into the UK, especially from the New Commonwealth. Two young girls of Indian origin, from Kenya and Uganda, aged fifteen and sixteen, enter the UK to progress with their A-level education in London. Their uncle and his Yorkshire wife, Aunty Anne in London, are their guardians. Later, they are joined by their mother. Their father luckily has the finances to buy a house for his family in High Wickham during the wave of anti-immigration that appears to have gripped the UK at the time. Their father joins them too and London, and later High Wickham, become the new family hub. The two teenage girls were my sister, Sabiha and me.

While my uncle and aunt provided us with the crucial support system that we required, the move from Uganda to England was by no means seamless. Sabiha and I had studied science in Uganda and wanted to continue our studies in that field. However, we found ourselves having to learn typing for accountancy and commerce instead, when we joined school in London. My mother came to our rescue then. She had completed her Senior Cambridge exams and had been in the midst of her medical degree in India just prior to the partition of India. When the situation in India became critical and dangerous, my grandfather asked my mother to return to Kenya. She was unable to complete her medical degree but went on to become a teacher in Kenya and had been instrumental in furthering our education. She therefore, was having none of this. She asked our school principal to move us from commerce to science and even asked them to test us on our knowledge of science. British colonies in general, followed a similar curriculum to that in the UK so that the level of education was the same throughout. But our school in London had not even bothered to see our academic results from our schooling in Kenya and Uganda and were clueless about the curriculum, syllabus, and level of education that we had received in both countries. We proceeded to surprise the headmistress with our good grades in the test they set for us in science. She was an astute woman and thereafter altered her thinking where students coming to UK schools from the Commonwealth was concerned. In fact, I used to be called into the admissions office when students from Commonwealth countries in Asia had their interviews, in case they were unable to understand the accents of those prospective students, in an attempt to make a fair and informative decision and ensure that no one was misjudged.

Getting our heads around the different accents of our teachers was a whole different experience. We had teachers with strong Scottish and New Zealand accents. Our English, learned in a British colony was very much the 'Queen's English'. Our first year in our new school in London provided us with a learning experience on more than just the academic front.

My sister went on to Imperial College for her degree but fell ill with toxic shock syndrome in her final year. This was when we moved to High Wickham to quieter surroundings. By this time my father had also left Africa and joined us in the UK. Keen to start working as soon as possible, he looked for jobs as a bus driver and the like. However, he was highly overqualified for such jobs. He was eventually taken on as a cashier in the shoe shop Kurt Geiger. Kurt Geiger was an Austrian Jew who had migrated to Australia. After World War II, he moved to London and opened one of the most exclusive shoe outlets at the time. Kurt Geiger soon realised that my father was overqualified for the job that he was doing and gave my father greater responsibilities given his proficiency in maths and accounts. Geiger and my father became close friends until the former sadly passed away. My father then became the stock manager for Kurt Geiger shoes for all its outlets in the UK and Europe after it had been taken over by House of Fraser. After my family moved to High Wickham, the commute to London for work for my father was of course much longer.

In the interim, I completed my A levels and went on to Canterbury to study for my degree and two years of teacher training. I began my studies in Canterbury in 1970 at a time when Canterbury was an excessively conservative town. The residents of the town were not keen on Asians or people of colour living in the town itself. Therefore, all students of colour were given accommodation by the University on campus itself. When I began teaching, I had to find accommodation in town. I recall so vividly being turned down instantly by the landlady when I went to see a room in a house that had been advertised. Some of the town residents at the time also objected to an Indian restaurant in town as they did not like the smells of spices and cooking emanating from it. In all of this however, we have to remember that firstly, it was the 1970s in England and secondly, this was not the mindset of all, but rather a minority.

Meanwhile, my brothers were facing the brunt of racism, bullying, and even violence in their school. They began leaning heavily towards the Socialist movement that was gripping England at the time and were actively involved in its activities. In fact, one of my brothers, who had joined City University, started the sit-in there to protest against the rise in tuition fees for foreign students. Due to this hike in fees, some of his friends had been unable to continue with their degrees as they could not afford the fees anymore. He also had no doubt about the institutional racism that was prevalent at the time and continued to fight for the rights of those who had been disadvantaged by government policies and actions. He had been at the forefront of some of the militant demonstrations along with Tariq Ali for instance. My father on the other hand, having been part of the Civil Service in Kenya refused to believe that the police in England could ever be discriminatory. He was convinced that they were upstanding officers of the law and was quite upset about my brothers' involvement in the Socialist movement.

My base by this time, had more or less become Canterbury. After teaching there for a year, I embarked on a PhD at the University. This was when I met my husband, Mushtaq, who was a Wellcome Trust student. Mushtaq had grown up in Uganda and had to flee with his family to the UK during Idi Amin's rule. His family were originally from Gujarat in India and belonged to the small Shia'h community of Bohras. Mushtaq's father had migrated to Uganda (Lira) in his teens and set up a general store there. However, his family knew Milton Obote and when Idi Amin overthrew Obote's government, he had to flee to the UK with his family. Mushtaq had excelled academically in Uganda and in his A levels. He accepted the offer from Sheffield University for his first degree, moving on to Canterbury for his Doctorate. He completed his PhD and proceeded to a Fellowship, also with the Wellcome Trust, in St. George's Medical School, where I joined him after graduating with my PhD. It was a research post for two years. His post could have been extended but we felt that we needed more stability. Neither of us wished to live in a big city.

Aberystwyth, Wales – 1984. A sleepy seaside university town at the end of the train line in Mid-Wales, the seat of the first University in Wales and the eminent professors who taught the then heir to the British throne, now King Charles III. A young couple, both scientists, obtain jobs in the Biochemistry Department at the University. The young man lectures in Human Biology and Biochemistry, while his wife is a part-time lecturer and researcher in the department. This young couple was my husband and me. The academic positions in what was then, the University of Wales, Aberystwyth was just what we had been looking for. I have lived in Aberystwyth now for almost forty years, since 1984.

Mushtaq became Senior Lecturer in the Biochemistry department and even had a few patents to his name, such as the one in gene engineering in 1993. I was happily busy with part-time lecturing in the department as well as research in the laboratory. We both felt that Aberystwyth was the right place for us and our son, Imran, who was born in 1988. My sister and my father joined us in Aberystwyth later. Sabiha arrived in 1990 after my mother's death, and became a second mother to my son. My father retired from Kurt Geiger in 1991 and followed soon after. On account of my other responsibilities – I looked after not only my young son and my father, but also was the primary carer for my sister – I preferred part-time lecturing contracts and laboratory research whenever time permitted. Even now, despite having retired, due to my lab experience, I am on hand to aid with experiments as and when needed.

The one large fly in the ointment was the manner in which Mushtaq and I were received, or rather felt discriminated against by a small minority in Aberystwyth. Mushtaq had come in as a new blood lecturer, brought in to revive and inject new life into a flagging and stagnant department, which, at times, caused a bit of friction. We felt like we had to work that bit harder to keep proving ourselves as productive and successful incomers before we were accepted fully.

For the first three years, before Imran came along, I used to go with Mushtaq to the laboratory, be it day or night, evenings or weekends as we had to keep a sharp eye on the experiments. If things went wrong or needed attention, especially in the case of bacteria which grows swiftly, it had to be dealt with instantly. Despite the long hours and hard work, we enjoyed it all since this was after all, our passion.

The years and decades passed by in Aberystwyth watching our son grow into a fine young man and all the while, we remained busy with our respective work commitments and my responsibilities at home, until our lives came to a shocking halt when Mushtaq passed away prematurely in 2010. We, as a family, got through our huge loss only due to the massive support we received from our neighbours, our close friends in Aberystwyth and in other parts of the UK. This included Mushtaq's and my PhD supervisors who have been staunch friends throughout our lives.

Sometimes, in our daily lives, it could be difficult to get involved in other activities, charities, organisations, and social networks outside the academic bubble, especially given our all-consuming dedication to the field of science. But having a child growing up in Aberystwyth and a sister who needed support meant that I got involved in summer school teaching as well as the mental health charity, Mind in Aberystwyth. Mind does sterling work and has been incredibly supportive and beneficial for Sabiha. When I was asked recently to join the Board of Mind, I agreed to it knowing that this was my chance to repay all the help and support it provided my family at a time when we needed it the most.

When Imran was in primary school, he returned home upset one day because one of the boys in his class told him he was the colour of 'poo'. After that the school requested me to talk to the schoolchildren about our culture, traditions, and customs. This proved to be a successful move and soon I was also asked to conduct similar talks in the other schools in and around Aberystwyth. In fact, I was part of the PTA at Imran's school, and we began the tradition of the annual barbeque and we held the first one in 1999. Imran faced occasional discrimination even at his secondary school, where I too used to take on some supply teaching from time to time. However, he did not let that perturb him and he had a strong core of firm friends, with whom he is still very close, despite now having moved to Gloucestershire with his wife and one-year-old daughter.

My one regret is that I never learned Welsh. Initially I had not felt the need to learn the language since everyone spoke English. Now I wonder if I would have felt even more integrated if I had also learned Welsh. Nevertheless, I do feel like I am fully a part of the Aberystwyth community. I have a very mixed group of friends, many of whom are Welsh too. I also find that the Welsh find it easier to follow the Indo-Kenyan accent, perhaps because of the similar lilt in the two accents. Wales, the Welsh people, the language, the culture, are all part of me now, and it will be incredibly difficult to leave Aberystwyth and Wales. The flip side is that my sister and I will be moving closer to Imran and his family and we will be able to enjoy seeing my granddaughter grow and be a part of her life at close quarters. Leaving Wales behind after nearly forty years will be a huge wrench, but at the same time, we are looking ahead to pastures new and a new chapter in our lives.

# 'The Good Life'

## Tomoko Holloway

I opened my eyes for the first time in my home on the outskirts of Tokyo, the city that runs on a firm ethic of hard work, efficiency, that relies on the punctuality of the Shinkansen (bullet train), and which is enveloped in the heady scent of the cherry blossom carpet in the spring. I knew this would always be my home where I grew up, but as I lived through my formative years, I also quickly knew that this would not be my only home forever. My world needed to expand beyond the boundaries of my country. I eagerly joined a home-stay exchange programme when I was in High School whereby I spent a month in Australia. This spell brought to the fore the realisation that the English we had been learning through textbooks was not enough and I was determined to apply for another exchange programme at a later date that would allow me to study English for at least a year. The opportunity to accomplish just that presented itself during my university years in Tokyo. The scheme allowed me to study Development Studies in the University of East Anglia (Norwich), where we explored global challenges such as poverty, climate change, ethnic and gender inequalities, and how we can change the world for the better.

This one year was a tough one. Not only was I grappling with my fluency in English, but also felt a bit isolated in and amongst largely local students. In many ways, the UK can be a rather reserved country and I always felt like the 'other' and not entirely accepted into the fold of local students. The saving grace was that I did make some good friends among other Japanese students and some foreign students also studying there. However, I had wanted to experience the full benefits of an 'exchange' programme where we could learn from other cultures and also impart some of our own culture. The difficult year nevertheless did not deter me – instead, I found that it was making me even more determined and resilient to make the most of this experience. I was also spurred on and heartened by the support and encouragement of my family in Japan. We had been a close-knit family, consisting of my parents, older sister, younger brother, and grandparents. Being away from them for a year in a different country was not easy, but this year away further tightened the familial bonds.

The most significant development in this one year, that would have lasting implications for me, was that I met my future husband (a student in his final year from the Norfolk/Suffolk area) at the University of East Anglia. Even before we met, he had been enamoured by Japanese culture and had already applied to a teaching programme promoted by the Japanese Government (The Jet Programme), whereby young graduates from various English-speaking countries went to teach English in Japan. Consequently, he followed me back to Japan just a few weeks after I had returned home having completed my year of study in Norwich. However, he was teaching in the north of Japan, and we still had to take flights to visit each other during his tenure there. While in Japan, he occupied the position of teaching assistant. His plan then was to return to Norwich, acquire his teacher training qualifications and return to Japan as a fully qualified teacher. But unfortunately, he did not get on well with the teacher training course and left not long after it had begun. He got a job thereafter in an estate agency and we got married soon after. Thus began my life in earnest in the UK as an immigrant.

The first couple of years were riddled with homesickness. I missed my family and close friends and always looked forward to visiting Japan as and when it was possible to do so. Returning to Norwich as a resident as opposed to a student was a completely different experience and I no longer knew anyone there. All the friends that I had made as a student, had also returned to their respective homes. The first few months therefore were terribly lonely ones and I found myself alone at home for much of the time. It was only when I was pregnant with my first child that I became acquainted with other Japanese mums, also married to Englishmen, through the Japanese Society. My world expanded greatly after I had my first child. I joined a few mother and baby groups locally and befriended other Asian and European mums, with whom I formed close bonds.

My world and my mindset also underwent a transformation while I was pregnant with my first child. My husband's aunt is a doula and she introduced us to the entire concept, the deeper understanding of the state of pregnancy and process of birth. She taught us about the autonomy that a couple has in deciding how the baby should come into the world. Prior to speaking to her we, like so many others, thought that our only option was to have a hospital birth. She suggested that I could opt to have a home birth since I was healthy, young, and a person of low risk. It was akin to the opening of a whole new world for us, and we felt empowered by it. I did eventually opt to have a home birth (water birth), something that worried my mother greatly as this was not a common occurrence in Japan. She had come over to be with us and to help us around the time of the birth and remained somewhat anxious about our decision until my son arrived safely into this world after a home birth. I felt I was so fortunate to have had this kind of support from my husband's aunt and knew I needed to forward this knowledge and feeling of empowerment on to others. This largely prompted me to become a doula too.

Having my children was an experience which eventually resulted in a boost of self-confidence as through them, I connected with many other people, and it broadened my world. Looking back, I feel that I had been very naïve when I came to live in Norwich on a permanent basis. Back then, I was not confident enough to be myself. I had wanted to be like and emulate other English people and not stand out as different. As my confidence grew, I found myself becoming bolder.

My husband, meanwhile, left his job at the estate agency after a few years and returned to his teacher training course and went on to teach in Norwich for a couple of years. But one of the main reasons behind him wanting to become a teacher was to teach English in different parts of the world, travel the world and absorb the culture of another country and gain valuable experiences of teaching in the Far East and South-East Asia. With this aim in mind, he applied to teach in Bangkok, and we moved there for two years. In many ways, living in Bangkok further boosted my confidence. While in England, I had been feeling inadequate, feeling that I was not good enough because I was not English myself. But in Bangkok, my husband and I were both part of an ex-pat community. In fact, I was not only able to forge links with the Japanese ex-pat community there, but also within the English ex-pat community since I spoke English. I realised that I did not have to be like other English people, but rather, I could use my knowledge of English as a tool to form friendships with other English ex-pats, while being an ex-pat myself. It was liberating to finally realise that I no longer felt the need to strive towards being someone or something I am not. Instead, I could be myself, the person I am with pride. We enjoyed our time in Bangkok, especially the culture and the food, but living in a big city and raising children in a city environment such as that of Bangkok was not for me. The quality of air was very poor, especially at certain times of the year and we did not want our children to grow up in a space with high levels of air pollution and therefore, potentially unhealthy surroundings. We wanted to be closer to nature and somewhere that was more rural.

My husband fortunately found a job in Guernsey as a teacher. I too had begun the training course to become a doula online towards the end of our stay in Bangkok. My youngest son was still very small and with me most of the time. This did not permit me too much free time to complete my course quickly and it was a slow process, given that we moved countries too during this spell. I eventually completed the course in my second year in Guernsey. I had always been clear that my priority was my children and training as a doula came second, as and when I had the time to progress with the course. Guernsey was the perfect place to explore and enjoy with my three boys, who also loved the abundant beaches and nature. This was where I took up sea swimming, something I continue to enjoy even in Wales.

While we loved the environment in Guernsey, at the same time, we felt that it was not really home. There appeared to be segregation between locals and incomers and on account of the nature of my husband's teaching contract, we knew that we could not stay there permanently. We needed to find the right place to finally put down our roots. We more or less stumbled upon the west coast of Wales by chance. After living in Guernsey, we could not imagine living somewhere too far from the sea, so we chose the beautiful coast of Wales. Initially we looked along the Pembrokeshire coast but did not find the right place. On the last day of our search, the house that we currently live in was shown to us in Pennant, which is a few minutes inland from the coastal town of Aberaeron. We can see the sea and beautiful sunsets from the hill behind our house and we have ample space outside to grow our own food. The plan is to keep chickens or ducks at some point too. We feel truly thankful to be living where we do. We enjoyed beautiful sunsets in Guernsey too, but here in Wales, we feel like we are able to soak in all the wonders of nature from our home.

Pennant feels even more like home because, even though we have only lived there for a couple of years, we were welcomed into the community almost straight away. In fact, the day after we moved into our new home, we were invited by our neighbours for their wedding anniversary celebration, which gave us the opportunity to instantly get to know the local residents. Never had we lived somewhere like this. In Norwich and Guernsey, we only had a passing acquaintance with our neighbours, but here, we were welcomed from the word go. We were also very fortunate to be introduced at this early stage to others of a similar mindset as ours. We got to know yoga teachers and wellbeing practitioners in the area. We met like-minded people who also felt a deep connection with nature, as we do – the feeling that there is power within us; something is moving us from within.

In Pennant and the surrounding area, we feel like we are in the gap between Aberystwyth and Cardigan, both of which are home to several events and groups. We wanted to set up groups and a community that focused on the connection with nature and physical, mental and spiritual wellbeing in an area where there isn't as much activity in this field. We began promoting our community, Aeron Valley Wellbeing Hub, on Facebook and our group consists of wellbeing practitioners in various fields such as yoga massage, dance, music, etc. My husband and I are two out of the five founding members of this group, and we try and organise community-focused events and activities in the area. For instance, during Christmas we run a Christmas wreath-making event and on a more regular basis, we have set up a food pantry, whereby all those who have an excess of the produce that they grow, can contribute it to the pantry. The pantry is almost like a community food stall which can benefit those who might need it or make use of the excess produce. Setting up our Wellbeing Hub took some time since we had to formalise the establishment of the project. It has been up and running since February 2022 and it is still early days – we are learning the ropes as we take each step ahead.

My doula practice is, in some ways, linked to the wellbeing community project but at the same time also quite separate since it is my own venture. In a relatively remote and at times, isolated part of the country, I am the only person supporting mums in the vicinity as a doula. In many ways, it is also an intergenerational prospect for many mums have the support of their families and local communities and I, as a doula, do not only provide individual support to the mum-to-be, but also to the people around her. However, the number of mums employing the services of a doula have been very few. The preconception is that it is largely the very affluent members of society who could afford the services of a doula. In a generally low-income area such as mid-west Wales, employing a doula is seen as a luxury. In many areas, there is funding that is available if mums-to-be wish to have a doula, but since April/May 2023, this funding has been temporarily stopped. As a result, I am still finding my feet in this field.

As a doula, support begins from the time a woman becomes pregnant. I then help them with prenatal education. I am not keen on the term 'education' in this context because I believe that pregnant women already have a good amount of knowledge about pregnancy and their own body instinctively. I like to think that I help mums to 'remember' that instinctive knowledge. Doulas are present during the birth of course, helping the mum through the birthing process (whether it is a home birth or in the hospital) and the support continues for a while even after the birth of the baby. In so many ways, mothers need as much support after the baby is born as they do during pregnancy. We believe that the mother has also given birth to herself as a mother, and she needs nurturing and support too. We try and help them to maintain the trust and confidence they have in pursuing the path that they have chosen. Many women feel vulnerable once they become pregnant and they are in need of love and support and the role of a doula is paramount in providing this. I believe that human beings are not designed to live solitary or isolated lives, especially if there are children involved. As the saying goes, 'It takes a village to raise a child'. I feel that it is important for mothers to have that support from the community and for the children to have that interaction with others outside the immediate nuclear familial network. The mind and the body are inextricably linked. While the medical team takes care of the physiological process of giving birth, a doula is providing the informational, practical, and emotional support.

In our new home in Pennant, we have been welcomed by our neighbours and the community, but ironically, most of them are also English or then people from outside Wales. Strangely enough, here too I feel like there is a kind of segregation between the native Welsh residents and incomers. My husband too is self-employed as a transformational life coach, Yoga teacher and Tai Chi instructor. He also facilitates creative dance and music sessions for self-expression with all populations such as those living with dementia, people with learning disabilities, elders, and children. However, with both of us being self-employed, we have found that it has taken a while for us to be accepted by local Welsh people in the area. It is clear that we need to keep going – we cannot expect immediate results. We are optimistic that with time, we will eventually be accepted by the native Welsh residents as long as we also show respect to their culture and language.

Due to our fairly mobile lifestyle in the past, my children have also had to get used to living in different countries, in and amongst different cultures and languages. They have been trying to imbibe the different school cultures as well, but my oldest son is feeling the brunt of it now. He is fourteen and as an adolescent, he is not too keen on learning yet another new language i.e. Welsh. He has just begun his GCSE subjects and had been keen on taking up the subjects that he is interested in. However, since Cymraeg is one of the subjects he has to take up, he has had to drop one of the subjects that he had been eager to pursue. He has been rather upset about this. He has the necessary resilience nevertheless and has made some good friends who are like-minded. Since he is the oldest, he has had to adjust the most as we moved from Norwich to Bangkok to Guernsey and now, Pennant. It was upsetting for me too to see him struggle initially to fit into his new school environments. My middle son has always been the most easy-going. He and my youngest son are now in the same school and that does make a difference to the adjustment process for them. It seems to have been a much more seamless process for my younger sons than it has been for my oldest son. However, we feel like we are now finally 'home' and hope that the three boys will fully settle in their new school environments and amongst their new peer groups.

Did I miss Japanese food when I first came to live in the UK? Yes, I certainly did – especially my mother's cooking. But now I find that commercial Japanese food tends to have more artificial flavourings and colour and neither I nor my stomach are keen on that. I still cook Japanese food at home, which is not authentic, but they tend to be relatively-easy and quick meals. I do not tend to buy too many Japanese ingredients anymore. While I do buy basic ingredients like soy sauce, I make my own Miso paste. I try and source as many local ingredients as I can for the food we consume at home as a family.

I feel that our journey in the past was necessary to discover myself. I still feel that my identity is Japanese, but I do not think I would have found peace if I still lived in Japan. I love going back to Japan to visit my family and friends, but I would no longer be able to adapt to life there, especially now that we have found our way in life. We have found autonomy through our journey, something I would not have experienced if I lived in Japan. In so many ways, Japan is still a patriarchal culture and women do not have the same levels of autonomy as we have here in the West. It may seem to the outsider that things are changing in Japan, but it is the mindset in its essence that needs to alter. While I have found a home in Wales, I feel like I have also lost my original home. Being self-employed as a doula has also made me a more resilient person and at the same time made me confident enough to be the person I am, rather than constantly feeling inadequate or feeling the need to become someone I am not in essence. It has been a journey I have enjoyed and continue to enjoy and through it, I, Tomoko Holloway, originally from Japan, married to an Englishman and now a doula in Wales, have flourished.

# 'The Beauty of Wales'

## Kamani Ranasinghe-Arachchige

A gentle tapping sound wakes me one damp afternoon from a nap. I walk to the window, draw the curtains and gaze out. A drizzle and mist in the distance hangs over the verdant green hills beyond. Am I in Ratnapura? No ... it can't be. As the sleepy haze lifts from my eyes and my consciousness, I remember ... I am in Wales now – in Pontypridd. But the vista is fondly reminiscent of my homeland, where I grew up.

I was born in Galle in 1955 and am the oldest of my siblings in my family. Galle, on the south-west coast of Sri Lanka, is an old town which is home to a fort, which was first built by the Portuguese in 1588 and later extensively fortified by the Dutch in the seventeenth century. It is now a UNESCO site. It was a traditional seaside town with lush coconut plantations. I floated through the first ten years of my life there seemingly as an echo of former colonial times and way of life – Sri Lanka having gained its independence only seven years prior to my birth. My family followed the British customs of wearing shoes and socks at home, servants around to take care of our needs and ample space around, in which to play.

When I was eleven, we moved to Ratnapura or Gem City which is situated in South Central Sri Lanka. It gets its name as it is the hub of the precious stones trade. Surrounded by lush mountains due to high levels of rainfall, it is no wonder that my current home of Pontypridd in Wales brings back memories of my early years in Ratnapura.

I obtained my education in missionary schools which taught both English as well as the local Sinhala language (since I am Sinhalese and therefore was part of the Sinhala stream) and fluency in both languages was natural and common. In fact, in Ratnapura there were also Tamil students and there was simultaneous education for Tamil students in the Tamil stream. There were no traces of any form of ethnic conflict at the time and both, the Sinhalese and Tamil residents coexisted peacefully.

Having topped my O levels, I was granted a place in a school in Colombo for highly gifted female students to study for my A levels. I received excellent grades even for my A levels and went on to Colombo Medical School to study Medicine. I performed well in the first two years but then fell ill during my third year. Fatigue and a fever overcame me for long spells which meant that I was unable to proceed with my studies. I was seen by doctors and psychiatrists, but my condition could not be diagnosed.

The silver lining through this uncertain time was the support I received from my boyfriend, who I had met during my A levels, while he was at university. We eventually got married in 1985. He was an Occupational Therapist at the School of Physiotherapy and Occupation Therapy and soon after we married, he won a WHO scholarship to visit hospitals in India, Delhi in particular.

The civil war was raging by this time, but much of the fighting was taking place in the north of the country, and the war did not directly impact us, especially in Ratnapura where I grew up. I have close Tamil friends in Ratnapura and even now, when we return there, we stay with them, and they prepare delicious Tamilian food for us.

Meanwhile, I continued to receive psychiatric treatment as my health predicaments were ongoing. One doctor noticed that there was possibly a thyroid abnormality and with appropriate doses of Thyroxin, I was able to rejoin a private medical school in Colombo and finally graduate despite the irregularities in my health and disruptions to my studies.

In 1994, the UK was recruiting occupational therapists from abroad and my husband's application was granted by the UK. His first place of work was near Merthyr Tydfil but I was unable to accompany him as I had, by this time, been granted a place in the private medical school in Colombo and was in the process of completing my medical degree. After graduating, I joined him in the UK, but by then he was posted In London. Once in London, I was presented with the opportunity to study further at Queen Mary University, but my persistent health issues prevented me from pursuing this path.

Things began looking up however, in the late 2000s when we moved to Wales. A private GP practice in Cardiff was brought to my attention and I was referred by the GP to a Consultant in Endocrinology and Diabetes. The Consultant explained that there was a problem with my T3 and asked if I would agree to try a form of medication that had not been administered to patients prior to this. At this point in my life, I had been feeling so unwell that I felt that I would not even make it through the next couple of months. My experience of GP consultations in London before this had been extremely unsatisfactory, unsympathetic, and unsuccessful in getting to the bottom of my medical condition. Disheartened and anxious, I had been plummeting into depression. I had been prescribed psychiatric medication which had a detrimental effect on me – I was unable to continue my further studies or to work and felt like I had wasted the medical qualifications that I had achieved despite my health struggles in Sri Lanka. Moving to Pontypridd and receiving focused, knowledgeable, and sympathetic medical attention from doctors in Wales proved to be the injection of hope and optimism that I had been seeking. It was my move to Wales that had created this positive shift. It is this monumental change in my outlook that my life in Wales had enabled, along with the natural scenery, that constitutes the beauty of Wales in my eyes.

The medication administered to me by my private consultant in Wales, took effect within two weeks and my GP surgery was asked to begin prescribing it to me on the NHS on account of the high costs I was incurring through private prescription. Since then, this medication has been made available free of charge in parts of Wales via the NHS and many other patients have benefitted from it too. My interactions with both the medical staff and the people in general here in Wales made me realise just how humble and welcoming a people they are.

On so many levels, my move to Wales has been my saving grace. We not only live amongst friendly neighbours, but also the community in general is genuine and accepting of us as incomers. I was told once by a lady I was chatting with that I should not think that the Welsh people are being overly nosey – they are just being friendly. Interactions with other Sri Lankans in Pontypridd and the surrounding area are limited – while there are quite a few Sri Lankan students in Cardiff, there are only a handful of Sinhalese and Tamil families in and around Pontypridd. The closest Buddhist temple is in Bristol and therefore not all that convenient for us to visit on a more regular basis. Sometimes, there are visiting Buddhist monks who are invited to give talks, but not very often. As a result, we do not celebrate Sri Lankan festivals here in Pontypridd as we would in Sri Lanka.

I have not been back to Sri Lanka since 2015 on account of my ill health. While I miss the sunlight that is abundant in Sri Lanka, especially during the long, dark winters here, I increasingly feel that Wales is now my home. It is the place where I am beginning to regain my health, my confidence, and my life. Prior to moving to Wales, I lived for ten years in London and even amongst throngs of people at all times, I felt lonely. Here in Pontypridd, I live in a relatively secluded area of five houses and families. I never feel lonely or afraid. My neighbours and the people in general are extremely helpful and I therefore am not reluctant to seek assistance if I require it.

Eating uninspired hostel food during my many years living in hostels in Sri Lanka, has not left me craving the food from back home. My husband, however, does miss Sri Lankan food and whipping up Sri Lankan dishes here in Wales is not a difficult task as most of the ingredients are available in supermarkets around us. We have also created our own version of Maldive fish, a dried fish used in numerous Sri Lankan dishes which is not readily available here. We drain a tin of tuna, add enough salt to cure it and spread it out in a pan over the fire. We store it and use it in dishes as we would Maldive fish. As they say, necessity is the mother of invention!

Living in Wales has benefitted me not only physically, but also mentally. Gaining the peace of mind in the knowledge that people will help me when I need help, has taken a weight off my shoulders. I have an emergency button given to me by the NHS, but I found the loop attached to it uncomfortable. Having explained my problem to the lady at the haberdasher's in town, I was extremely touched when she instantly assured me that it could be fixed easily, and simply took it off my hands, attached a woollen loop to it that could go around my neck and handed it back to me without batting an eye. It is these gestures that I encounter on a regular basis in Wales that I find tremendously kind and touching. When I lived in London, the days seemed to simply pass by in a blur, but here in Pontypridd, I can sit back and truly appreciate my surroundings and feel safe and incredibly fortunate. One should never underestimate safety. So much anxiety often stems from feeling unsafe. Once we feel safe, we automatically start feeling that little bit less anxious and more confident.

I used to write poetry a few years ago. I had regular chats with a Cognitive Behavioural Therapist in Wales, who also happened to be Buddhist, and at one time, he asked me to write a poem to express my current emotions. The poem I wrote was read thereafter anonymously during their annual meeting. At the time, I was at a low point. Thoughts about how different my life could have been if I had not been put on wrong psychiatric medication, had been foremost in my mind. If I had not been on this medication, I perhaps could have carried on with my further studies in Medicine and I

might have been able to pursue a fulfilling working life. In this frame
of mind, I had lost the confidence to have my poem presented in the
public sphere in my name, which is why it was read anonymously.
How things have changed since moving to Pontypridd! Now I have
the confidence to share my poems here for all to read.

**Antidote for Pain**
Is it revenge?
Is it running away?
Or fighting back?
Or antidote for pain is,
Courage to stand up;
And courage to accept?

The antidote for pain is love
The unconditional self-love,
To love who I am,
No matter what I am.

The antidote for pain is forgiving,
The courage to accept, And, courage to forgive,
All who took my dreams away.

**Mending**
Mending is a difficult job,
It takes lot of time,
Needs lot of patience And, so much courage too.

Courage to live,
Courage to survive, Gives courage to mend,
Day by day, hour by hour,
With trial and error,
New ways of learning,
We all see the light.

Triumph of joy,
Music of the Band!!!
Smile and songs!!!!
Oh!! We all are at the other end of the tunnel!!!!

The poems I wrote reflect my low point. I felt cheated of my ambitions, my dreams, and my plans for the future. I had realised that I had been wrongly given psychiatric medication which hindered my dreams. I only wrote ten poems at the time, but each one is from the heart and similar in sentiment. Every time I wrote a poem, I used to ring my mother and read it out to her as I valued her response and comments immensely.

With the Cognitive Behavioural Therapy that I received, came the much-needed and long-overdue encouragement to write poetry, to pick up the pieces and move on with my life with a positive stance. People are encouraging me to add to my poetry collection and publish them in a book. It truly gladdens my heart to know that my poetry is being appreciated.

In 2018, I was diagnosed with Functional Neurological Disorder, which manifests Itself in neurological symptoms stemming from the nervous system. The neurological condition has also impacted my vision. I have double vision and find reading difficult. I am therefore registered with The Royal National Institute of Blind People, Wales (RNIB) which keeps an eye on me and is helping me along the way.

Even before my condition had been diagnosed, I had been receiving PIP (Personal Independence Payment) for my hitherto undiagnosed condition which resulted in frequent headaches and tiredness. But when my PIP award ran out in 2016, it left me financially vulnerable. I struggled to reapply for PIP and remained unsuccessful. In 2019, the Department for Work and Pensions revisited me, but failed to even peruse my medical records. Due to the anxiety caused by my medical condition, I find it difficult to speak with people in person and communicate effectively. Finally, I browsed the internet to seek advice and came across The Brain Charity. The help I received from the charity proved to be invaluable and my PIP was reinstated in 2021 until 2029.

They used my story as an example of how The Brain Charity has been successful in aiding people like me, who struggle each day against bureaucracy. I am now in a safe environment with happier prospects, a helpful community, appropriate treatment for my medical condition and financial security. With much of the external triggers for my anxiety absent, I can finally look ahead with hope and positivity.

Kamani's experience of PIP and help from The Brain Charity can be found at: https://www.thebraincharity.org.uk/story/functional-neurological-disorder-pip/

# Here, There and Everywhere: The Long Journey to Wales

**Lynda Williams**

In a way, my journey began with the journey my maternal grandparents made from The Netherlands to what was then Rhodesia, now Zimbabwe. They bought a dairy farm in Rhodesia and raised cattle. I recall spending my early childhood running about on the farm and learning to milk cows by hand. My parents, siblings and I did not live on the farm – we lived in the second-largest city, Bulawayo where I was born. Sadly, my father passed away when we were very young and although my mother remarried, she was largely responsible for our upbringing. My mother was, and has always been a music teacher in school. However, when the Rhodesian Bush War or the Zimbabwean War of Liberation, which had been ongoing since 1964, took on a fierce intensity in the latter part of the 1970s, we had no choice but to pack everything up and move to South Africa. From what I recall, there was definitely an urgency to our departure from Rhodesia. I think my grandparents had their farm confiscated, which broke my grandfather's heart, and once we had finally settled in South Africa in the town of East London, they came to live with us. My mother had converted the garage into living accommodation for them and bought chickens to keep them company. Like every other South African home, which was essentially a detached bungalow, we had a garden and a pool that we had installed ourselves. The more affluent section of society tended to have two-and three-storey homes, but the average South African homes were bungalows. My grandfather (Opa), who had been an engineer back in The Netherlands, eventually died of asbestos poisoning, but my grandmother (Oma), being of strong Dutch stock, lived to a good age.

Initially, we lived in many different towns in South Africa after our move there. In fact, I think that I moved schools eight times in the formative twelve years of my schooling. Consequently, much of that period of my childhood is rather hazy in my memory. One of my strong recollections is that we were always outdoors playing with many other children. There were no other distractions then such as computers or televisions and therefore, we spent a very physically active childhood interacting with other children, something that can be quite uncommon in today's day and age, especially in the cities. It was a fairly patriarchal society on the whole. While my younger brothers went surfing, girls were not encouraged to surf. We usually hung about on the beach ready with towels for when the guys finished surfing. This was just the way it was then, and our upbringing was along these lines.

When we moved to East London, my mother became the Head of the Music Department in school and found it difficult to keep on top of the heavy workload and the responsibility of looking after four children on a daily basis. We were sent off to boarding school and I spent the rest of my school years in boarding school in King Williamstown, about thirty to forty minutes away from East London. The immense value and emphasis placed on education in our family perhaps stemmed from the fact that my mother herself is not only well-educated and has always been a music teacher in schools, but also because education was considered by her as holding us in good stead no matter where life took us. When my mother was just sixteen, she won a scholarship to the Royal Schools of Music in London and she successfully navigated her way through her time in London, despite not knowing a word of English when she arrived. Even though I hated my first couple of years in boarding school due to its strict rules after having had a free existence until then, I soon realised the value of the good education that I was receiving at the school and was then determined to make the most of what the school had to offer. My school not only instilled in me a firm sense of discipline, but also placed at my disposal a number of opportunities that I took advantage of, such as being part of the choir, debating society and sports (I was captain of the netball team), aside from excelling at my studies. I believe that I was the first student to be awarded badges for culture, academics, and sports and it was viewed as a significant achievement at the time.

I knew no Afrikaans when we moved to South Africa, since obviously it was not spoken in Rhodesia. Even though my mother is Dutch, my father, who was English, had forbidden my mother to speak to us in Dutch. He did not want us speaking in a language he could not understand and with hindsight, I feel it was a real shame – at that young age, we would have picked up Dutch quickly and easily. Nevertheless, I did manage to learn Afrikaans fairly quickly and am still fluent in it. At the time, schools in South Africa taught English and Afrikaans equally to a fairly high level. I chose not to simply stick to learning standard grade Afrikaans, but rather, higher-grade Afrikaans, which included Afrikaans literature. Once I knew Afrikaans, I found it easier to understand Dutch due to the similarities in the two languages. In addition, since we were in the eastern part of South Africa, we were also taught its regional language Xhosa to a certain degree.

After finishing my A levels, I went on to study for a degree in Marketing and Public Relations at the University in Port Elizabeth. The student loan system in South Africa was quite different from the system in the UK. Since my mother did not have the means to put us through university, my sister (who also did her teacher training in Port Elizabeth) and I put ourselves through university. I managed to procure a few bursaries and academic scholarships which made it feasible for me to pursue my degree. I completed my degree in 1991 and returned home to temp for about six months, just to save enough money for a one-way ticket to the UK. As a rule, Australians, Kiwis, and South Africans are encouraged to spend a year away since these countries are in the furthest reaches of the world. Since my father was British, I had taken advantage of my heritage and got myself a British passport. This made it easier for me to arrive in the UK in June 1992 after having saved enough money from my temp job. Ironically, South Africa had allowed us to apply for British passports since our father had been British, even though he had passed away when I was still a baby, but it did not allow us to apply for a Dutch passport even though my mother is Dutch and still living. This was a reflection of the patriarchal system in South Africa – maternal lineage and heritage did not hold the same weight.

Regardless, one of the best things I did was to get a British passport since it made the process of entering the UK so easy. I had intended to stay here only for my year-out. Nevertheless, I had sold my possessions in South Africa before I came to the UK, on a one-way ticket and with only about £300 to my name.

I made London my base, and stayed with a schoolfriend who was working in a pub in North London for a couple of weeks. In due course, I managed to get a job and then moved into my own flat and continued living in London for the next decade. It was a very difficult move for me in the beginning. London was a huge culture shock and I missed home. I shed many a tear in my early days in London. Contrary to my original plan to work for a while and then travel a little, I ended up taking up a permanent job in order to pay the bills. I had arrived in London during a recession and therefore, I could not have turned down a permanent job in that climate.

In all that time, I visited South Africa only once to see my family. While I had missed my family, I also knew that I could never live in South Africa. I had grown up in South Africa during the apartheid and left it just before Nelson Mandela was released from prison. My formative years were marred by segregation and discrimination which upset me greatly. I remember going to beaches which were divided into three sections, the best part of it for the white residents, the section that was kind of acceptable, for the Indian residents and the worst, almost dangerous section with broken glass, etc., for the African people. This was not an environment in which I wanted to live long-term. My mother had always brought us up to treat people with respect, and the unfairness and discrimination I witnessed did not gel with my upbringing and strong notion of fairness and equality. Having said that, the UK too was by no means, and still isn't, anywhere near perfect, but comparatively, it seemed to me that people of colour had a few more opportunities in the UK, than in the South Africa of the apartheid era that I had left behind.

My time in London was also a pivotal period in my life for it was through work that I met my husband, John, who hails from Barnet in London/Hertfordshire. We got married in 1998. However, a few years later, when we decided to start a family, we felt that London was not the right place to raise children. John's father had lived in Bronant, a hamlet in the county of Ceredigion in mid Wales for quite a few years and we decided to go there too to gauge if we could possibly move to the same area. We decided to give Aberystwyth a go, although I struggled with this decision. I had been a city girl through and through and felt that Aberystwyth was the back of beyond.

Back in London, John had a garden and landscaping business and we had also invested repeatedly in properties that needed a full renovation, would sell them and buy bigger properties with the same aim. In this way, we had managed to accumulate a few savings. Those were the days when one could double one's money, but not anymore. Both our families had not been very well-off and therefore, we didn't have very much at the start in terms of capital. Additionally, since I had a stable job, I was able to get a mortgage, whereas since John was self-employed, he had been unable to procure a mortgage. As a result, we had been able to not only buy a house to live in in London, but also a flat which we rented out. In London, we had struggled to fall pregnant, probably because I was overworked and underweight. I had also had a miscarriage. Perhaps it was the right time when we moved to Aberystwyth, for I became pregnant a month after we moved there, and my daughter was born in late 2002. The house that we moved into is now the vicarage for St. Anne's Church in town. We sold it to the church, and it has been the vicarage ever since. Meanwhile, John had bought two derelict barns near Llanrhystud, which needed full revamps but none of them were ready by the time we sold our house. The church very kindly rented us a house for about eight months in Llanfarian which came with a donkey named Charlie, which also happens to be the name of my son, born in 2004 and which both my children loved. When one of the barn conversions was ready, we moved into it while John worked on the other one. Then we sold the first one and moved into the second one once it was ready.

Once both barns were sold, we couldn't see another project on the horizon in the area. While we were in London, my sister and brother had also come to live in London for a few years, but in 2002, my sister emigrated to New Zealand, while my brother remained in London. A few years later, my mother too emigrated to New Zealand from South Africa. Consequently, we began entertaining the idea of also emigrating to New Zealand if we felt it was the place for us. We moved there in 2007 initially on a six-month tourist visa. When it came to applying for a residence visa, we found that I qualified for the points system visa since I have a degree, whereas John did not. This meant that, contrary to what we had initially planned, I had to go to work full-time, and John took over the role of Mr. Mom, looking after the children full-time. It was quite a learning experience for us. In so many ways, New Zealand at the time, seemed to be still stuck in the 1970s. When John turned up at school to drop the children off and pick them up, the other mums were not too sure what to make of that. They were also rather hesitant to allow their children to come over to our house with a man in charge, so the situation was tricky and uncomfortable. The renovation industry there is also heavily taxed and that made it difficult for John to make a living from that, despite him managing to buy, renovate, and sell three properties during our time in New

198

Zealand. In general, even though we were in a country whose official language was English and it should have felt familiar, it was in fact, quite a culture shock for us. We decided then that New Zealand was not going to work out for us. To top it all, John, who had never lived anywhere else but in the UK, and is close to his family, especially his grandmother, felt the distance enormously. He began to appreciate the type of adjustment and compromises that I had made in moving from South Africa to the UK.

There was some debate about whether we should return to Aberystwyth or move to Cornwall. However, by then, I had had enough of starting from scratch. The year 2009 saw us back in Aberystwyth. We rented a flat while we looked for a house to buy. We finally bought the house in which we live now. My youngest son was born here in 2011 and this house is the only one he has ever known, whereas my older children had lived in numerous houses and in a different country on the other side of the world. This house and location are the longest that I have ever lived in. Besides, I had kept in contact with the friends that I had made from our previous stint in Aberystwyth, and I slipped straight back into life here, as did my children.

Ironically, while in London, we had everything at our disposal, but in order to live and survive in London, I had to work all the time. In our free time, the last thing I wanted to do was go back into Central London. I became pregnant almost as soon as we moved to Aberystwyth, and it was the first time that I had not been working in years. Even during my university years, I had been working in order to put myself through university. I had the most marvellous pregnancies in Aberystwyth and was able to have two home births with two midwives at my disposal. I began to appreciate my situation and my surroundings. Where else would I have had this level of relaxation and calm at a time when pregnant women need it the most? There is also something to be said about living by the sea. Apart from London, I had always lived by the sea and taken it for granted. However, when I lived away from the sea, I missed it terribly. Additionally, when children are young, Aberystwyth seems to have everything that they would need. We are also incredibly fortunate to have the Arts Centre here with a myriad of cultural events and shows by international artists. It is an international town on account of the university and the hospital, and we are lucky to be living in such a multicultural environment, despite being so remote. My mother had always encouraged us to explore the world and be open to others, a maxim that I am also able to live by even in a small town like Aberystwyth.

I have also tried to instil the same manners and sense of discipline that I received from my mother and my school in my own children. Being successfully self-employed, also calls upon my principle of discipline. Along with a property portfolio that I manage, John and I own an antique shop in town and when you have your own business, the buck stops with you. My priorities therefore are very clear when I am working from home – after my children, work comes first. After years of hopping from one place to another, we feel very settled here on all fronts – work, family, friends, neighbours, and social life. Simultaneously, I like the fact that I always meet people I know when I go into town, and yet, I don't know everyone I see. I like that balance. I am not sure I would have liked to live in a smaller town where everyone knows everyone else's business. I do sometimes feel a bit guilty that I haven't managed to learn Welsh in all these years of living in Aberystwyth and am unable to converse with clearly Welsh-speaking customers in our shop in Welsh. For the most part though, people are generally very friendly, welcoming, and courteous. My children, however, have been benefitting from learning Welsh at school from an early age.

As an immigrant, I find the issue of immigration a very complex one in the UK. I am very aware that as a white South African English-speaking immigrant, I have had an easier ride. For me, it is an accident of birth which I cannot help, but it does not stop me from seeing what is problematic around me.

As someone who came into the UK to work from another

country, I feel like my life is clearly divided into two halves. The years from zero to twenty-one years of age is my South African half, whereas the years from twenty-one to now is my UK half. I also feel incredibly sad when I think back on Rhodesia when I was a child there. It was a wonderful place to be, but since then, Zimbabwe has spiralled into a horrific situation. When people ask me, 'where are you from?', I find that question very difficult to answer. There is almost a sense of dichotomy in expressing who I am. Born in Rhodesia, but schooled in South Africa, Dutch mother, English father and husband, Welsh children and lived for a few years in New Zealand but essentially, more than half my life in the UK. What does that make me? Global? Or just plain lucky.

# The World is My Oyster

## Matluba Khan

I was born in a small town approximately seventy kilometres north of Dhaka, the capital city of Bangladesh. I am the youngest of five children – four sisters and a brother. I grew up feeling that the sky is the limit for me. My father, a teacher of language and art and superintendent of a Primary Teachers' Training Institute, made me believe there is no limit to which I can aspire and what I can achieve. I moved to Dhaka at the age of fifteen for my higher secondary education in a leading women's college. It was only later on, while studying architecture in the top Engineering and Architecture University of the country that I realised that my upbringing was not the norm but an exception in a typical Bangladeshi family. As a young woman, I exercised freedom to live my life on my own terms and I was enabled by my family to exercise agency in choosing the field in which I wanted to build my career. This was certainly a 'privilege' but something that was not earned through wealth but by the progressiveness and wisdom on the part of my late father. 'The world is your oyster; with self-determination and hard work you can achieve whatever you want to in life' – this is what my father used to tell me often.

I always wanted to travel the world and be a citizen of the world, exploring new cultures, countries, and places. I cherished the desire to be Ibn Battuta, travel the world and write about my journeys. I was often reminded by others how unsafe the world was for solo female travellers. They were not wrong in most cases, however, I did not let these perceived risks come in my way of finding a place in the world, travelling across Bangladesh and other parts of South Asia. My father always inspired me to become an independent woman, emotionally and financially, to be able to make my own decisions and take ownership of any decisions no matter what the outcome was.

I began my career as an associate architect in a leading architecture firm in 2009, and shortly after in the same year, I joined the same university that I graduated from, as a lecturer in Architecture. I was ready to embrace what life had in store for me when I arrived in Edinburgh in 2013 to pursue my PhD in landscape architecture. I was open to the challenges, uncertainties and the wonders of living in a new place thousands of miles away from what I knew as 'home'. That perhaps helped me see things differently, appreciate the differences and acknowledge the surprise, contempt, fear or dismay in people's eyes as they looked at me and my clothing and heard my accent. It also enabled me to take risks during my PhD and post-doctoral life as I transgressed the disciplinary boundary and decided to walk the intersection of disciplines and accepted a research position at the department of epidemiology and public health and moved to London.

I worked on a European Union research project run by a multi-country, multidisciplinary consortium comprising eighteen partner institutes from twelve countries throughout Europe. Soon I found myself not only as the only researcher with an architecture/built environment research background, but also the only person of colour in a team of more than thirty-five researchers. I was passionate about the work I was doing, and my contribution was appreciated as a driving force for the project.

While I cherish the positive outcomes and memories of my PhD and post-doctoral work, I have not quite moved past the negative experiences. On reflection, I wonder whether it was my workaholic attitude or naïveté that made me overlook the subtle, and on occasion, obvious racism that I experienced in professional or social environments. While I am grateful to my supportive and friendly colleagues, I often wonder why some of them remained silent at the sight of an obvious racist incident. Perhaps it was because I did not stand up for myself.

**When the world stood still...**
I moved to Wales in December 2019 taking the job of a lecturer at a Welsh university. Soon after, the whole world came to a standstill due to the outbreak of COVID-19. I was in a new city, new neighbourhood, and new workplace with new responsibilities and with a different set of procedures and protocols. In March 2020 with the enforcement of lockdown, teaching and learning moved online. Before I had managed to connect with colleagues and find my feet in the new department, we were exiled in our little home severing our connection with the world. Everyone in academia faced this challenge, however for me, leading and teaching non-traditional courses that involved design and project work brought unique challenges.

I terribly missed bumping into colleagues in university corridors when I could run my thoughts and concerns and doubts past them and ask someone to help with anything that I felt unsure about. I think while people found themselves productive when working from home, they also soon started to realise that not everything can be done over email, through Microsoft Teams or Zoom calls. Like most people, I craved company and socialisation in open spaces.

What I was experiencing at work was accentuated by my personal circumstances. My father-in-law died in Bangladesh on 17 March, the week before the lockdown and my husband was devastated at not being able to travel and be with his family. All this happened before he could find himself a new job and settle down in a new place, and he struggled with depression as did I with anxiety associated with academic and personal pressures.

I am not sure whether my experiences would have been different had I lived in another country or city. I despised commuting while living in London, so we found a flat at walking distance from my workplace in Cardiff. I also have a spacious office only to myself in the department contrary to the open-plan jam-packed office of the London university. All that I had planned and looked forward to enjoying, became something that was temporarily just beyond my grasp. Yet there was one thing that made a difference amidst all these challenges – the proximity of Bute Park to both my home and my department in Cardiff. My husband and I started making the most of our exercise within the five-mile distance from home, by walking in the park, exploring its nooks and crannies, strolling along the nature reserve and taking notice of the ducklings that swam from the Taff to the narrower streams of the park. We were fortunate to have been living in an area that had access to this resource, as I know many people living in apartments did not have any access to green spaces or nature, and many were scared to leave their homes.

**Friends in need...**
Another thing that made a difference was my colleagues (who soon became friends) and the socially distanced walks in Bute Park, along the Taff Trail and the Cardiff Bay Barrage with them (when the lockdown was eased to allow for people of two different households to meet outside). My colleague and friend, Amanda (name changed), invited me for a socially distanced walk in the park, which was the start of many socially distanced walks, and picnics (when allowed). We bonded during those walks, and I had the opportunity to share my concerns and worries and get the advice of a colleague on issues I found hard to address on my own.

The friendships kindled during that time continue today, and we continue to go for walks, enjoy organised picnics in parks, write together in the cosy comfort of cafés, and lend one another our shoulders when any of us go through a difficult time. My friends come from all over the world including parts of Wales, who have all found a home in Cardiff.

## 'Welsh Not' and International Mother Language Day

Before experiencing Welsh nature and friendships, what connected me to Wales was the Welsh language. No, I did not have any prior knowledge of Welsh and Welsh history, nor did I know how to read or write Welsh. I have developed an awareness of the language by undertaking a mandatory Welsh Language Awareness online course as my job requirement. This is a course with which I engaged with much enthusiasm and curiosity. I felt a certain affinity as I found some resemblance in the struggle that my compatriots have faced and endured to retain *Bangla* as the state language of then East Pakistan. *Bangla* has become the official language through bloodshed (on 21 February 1952) which culminated in the birth of the country named Bangladesh (literally meaning, the land of *Bangla*) in 1971. The United Nations have declared 21 February as International Mother Language Day as a tribute to the language movement of Bangladeshis and to promote the awareness of linguistic and cultural diversity and the notion that multilingualism can advance inclusion with regards to access to education.

My heart ached as I read about the 'Welsh Not' practice in schools and how mercilessly children were discouraged from learning and speaking Welsh. The Welsh language has come a long way with the enforcement of the Welsh Language Act 1993 and Welsh Language Measure of 2011. Although it is not always easy to uphold the Welsh Language Standards and the university's commitment to bilingual communication, I appreciate the measures undertaken. I think Bangladesh and Wales can learn a lot from each other and Bangladesh needs to consider their strategies in upholding *Bangla* Language Standards and ensuring the use of *Bangla* at all levels, along with recognising the languages of the indigenous population. I often wonder why *Bangla* is not the medium of instruction in state universities in Bangladesh. But perhaps that is the topic of discussion for another time.

207

**Working with the community I am part of…**

In summer 2021 we started to see some light at the end of the tunnel following mass vaccination, ease of restrictions on travel and resuming face-to-face activities. Local authorities started working on recovery strategies for 'building back better' as we came out of the pandemic. With my research interest in co-design with children and young people and community engagement, I wanted to work with the Cardiff community. I was part of the move towards capturing the voices of children and young people in devising recovery strategies for their neighbourhoods. Children's opinions are seldom asked for in planning and design of any recovery strategy, even though they are one of the most impacted segments of the community. Therefore, I developed a project with colleagues to work with children and young people from under-represented and marginalised communities of Cardiff to co-create a recovery plan for their neighbourhoods. The project in the first instance, focused on Grangetown, an inner Cardiff community with which the university has an established relationship and of which I think myself a part, living not far from the locality.

This project, funded as a civic mission project of the university, provided me with this incredible opportunity of learning about the lived experiences of children and young people, and how the pandemic has affected them. We partnered with the local authority and worked together to co-create a children and young people's plan for Grangetown, with short-, medium-, and long-term ideas to make Grangetown a child-friendly community. This project helped me connect with the community members, and work closely with girls and young women, understanding their challenges, needs, and preferences. Children and young people thought that spaces for girls and young women and play opportunities for disabled children should be a priority for action in any new dimension of the recovery plan.

## Spaces for young women...

Working with young women, I have come to learn about the challenges and inequalities they face in Welsh communities, particularly in Cardiff. This made me reflect on my experience of growing up in Bangladesh. While a lot of things are different in these two contexts, I was taken by surprise by the similarities in what girls and young women face in their everyday lives across the globe. The young women I have worked with, come from different backgrounds, but a majority are from immigrant families, whose parents or grandparents have come to Wales to find a home here.

Our research with young women highlighted the inequalities in design and planning of public spaces in Wales (and the world). It made me reflect on the fact that our neighbourhoods are designed/planned by able-bodied white male planners, and they often disregard the needs of children, the disabled, the elderly, and women, and they rarely ask for their preferences. Most parents thought that public transport and neighbourhood environments were unsafe for their daughters to be able to roam around independently or spend time with peers. It was interesting to learn from conversations with my male colleagues and friends that what they think is safe (a quiet alley on a weekend evening), could be perceived as unsafe by their partner/wife. Similarly, my husband is unwilling to go out or disapproves of me doing so to the city centre on a weekend evening. This is something I find quite interesting. The cities change during weekends and evenings, as people's behaviour can alter quite markedly with enough drinks in them.

The one thing that was quite surprising to me here in the UK (and it is sometimes difficult to disentangle the difference between the devolved nations) is the perceptions towards teenagers, and young men and women. Teenagers with the ongoing changes in their mind and body find it difficult to adapt to their surroundings while trying to find an identity of their own, but at the same time, society tends to be rigid with regards to designing adaptable spaces for them. The term 'teenagers' was introduced in America at the beginning of the twentieth century. In order to channel young, adolescent boys' energy properly, team sports were introduced in playgrounds to prepare for service to the country, while young girls were supposed to remain in their homes, preparing for the role of wives and mothers. While things have changed since then, young women still could find themselves designed out of public spaces, whereas adolescent boys/young men occupied the sports fields in an attempt to negotiate a space for themselves.

I am continuing my work with children and young people in Wales with my colleagues. Next year we will conduct a survey to explore parents' perception of girls' and young women's experience of public spaces and organise workshops to co-design public spaces with girls and young women. I am passionate about making public spaces in Wales more accessible to women, working with the community and the local authority, and contribute to the best of my ability towards making the world a better place for women.

**Finding a home in Wales...**

My husband and I found a home in Wales after a fair share of travelling all around the world. We love living in Cardiff, and we have enjoyed our four years here. I am grateful for what this city has offered me in this brief period of time. By the city, I refer to my wonderful colleagues and friends who lend their shoulders when I am going through hard times, Bute Park, the Taff Trail, Pen-y-fan, the Grange Pavilion, KIN + ILK Pontcanna, the Secret Garden Café, the Pembrokeshire Coastal Path ... and I want them to be a part of my life for much longer. We are in the process of buying our first home in Cardiff. Being trained as an architect and a landscape designer, I have all sorts of ideas to design our garden and I am, for now, reining in my thoughts and ideas until we get the key!

# About the Editor

Faaeza Jasdanwalla-Williams, originally from Mumbai, India, is a historian of women in the Ottoman Empire in the Early Modern Period and of the African Diaspora in India. She not only has publications relating to the African Diaspora, but has also participated in events and conferences held by the UN, the Afrikansk Kulturinstitutt in Oslo and the Schomburg Centre for Black Culture in New York. After completing her Doctorate from Aberystwyth University, she went on to teach in the Department of History at Aberystwyth University for ten years. She stepped down from teaching immediately prior to the COVID pandemic and soon after joined Honno as a Committee Member in 2020. Since then, she has been working closely with Honno on this project as the editor, as well as on the Script Committee. She is multilingual, including Welsh, which she learnt in an attempt to understand the culture of the country in which she currently lives, more closely.

# About the Co-compilers

Chinyere Chukwudi-Okeh, originally from Nigeria, is currently resident in Swansea and is closely involved with the African Association there, which is not limited to aiding African people, but also helps asylum seekers and refugees from other countries. She is a writer and recently completed her Masters in Creative Writing from Swansea University. She joined Honno on a temporary basis to help forge direct links with immigrant and migrant communities throughout Wales and encourage women from these communities to engage with this project and contribute their stories.

Mohini Gupta, originally from New Delhi, India, has just submitted her thesis on pedagogy and language teaching in India and Wales for a DPhil from Oxford University. She has been closely connected with Wales since she won the Charles Wallace Fellowship at Aberystwyth in 2017. She writes poetry in Hindi and has also been learning Welsh. She is the co-editor, along with Andrew Whitehead, of a Honno publication titled *The Hindu Bard*, published in 2023. She too joined Honno on a temporary basis to work specifically on this project, forging direct links with immigrant, migrant and refugee communities.

## ABOUT HONNO

Honno Welsh Women's Press was set up in 1986 by a group of women who felt strongly that women in Wales needed wider opportunities to see their writing in print and to become involved in the publishing process. Our aim is to develop the writing talents of women in Wales, give them new and exciting opportunities to see their work published and often to give them their first 'break' as a writer.

Honno is registered as a community co-operative. Any profit that Honno makes is invested in the publishing programme. Women from Wales and around the world have expressed their support for Honno. Each supporter has a vote at the Annual General Meeting. For more information and to buy our publications, please visit our website www.honno.co.uk or email us on post@honno.co.uk.

Honno
D41, Hugh Owen Building,
Aberystwyth University,
Aberystwyth,
Ceredigion,
SY23 3DY.

We are very grateful for the support of all our Honno Friends.